Knowledge and Responsibility

ISLAMIC PERSPECTIVES
ON SCIENCE

CONTRIBUTORS

- ABASI KIYIMBA graduated from Makerere University in Uganda, did his postgraduate work at the School of Oriental and African Studies (London) in Bantu oral literature, and is now teaching at Makerere University.

- M. FETHULLAH GÜLEN is an Islamic scholar and thinker and a prominent activist in interfaith dialogue and the promotion of education.

- ALI ÜNAL studied theology and English language and literature, and taught English at various high schools for many years. He writes for *Zaman*, Turkish daily newspaper, and is currently doing editorial work and writing for *The Fountain* and translating major Turkish works on religion, science, and culture into English. He is the author of several books in this field, published in both Turkish and English.

- YAMINE MERMER graduated from Algiers University with a degree in theoretical physics and did post-graduate work for her MSc and PhD degrees at Durham University, UK. Fluent in Arabic, French, English and Turkish, she has translated and published in several languages.

- SALIH ADEM is a two-times International Physics Olympiad (IPHO) gold medallist (1993 USA and 1995 Australia) and winner of the youngest participant prize in IPHO history (1992 IPHO). He participated in 4 international physics Olympiads successively (a world record). He has an MSc on biophysics (University of Illinois at Urbana Champaign) and an MA on philosophy (University of Maryland).

- M. SAIF ISLAM received his M.S. and a Ph.D. in Electrical Engineering from the University of California-Los Angeles (UCLA) in 1999 and 2001, respectively. Dr. Islam is the principal investigator of the Integrated Nanodevices and Systems Research (i-nano) of UC Davis, and has authored or co-authored more than 70 journal and conference papers and holds two patents with more than 30 pending patents as inventor or co-inventor.

- SUAT YILDIRIM is one of Turkey's leading theologians. He served as a mufti before pursuing a distinguished academic career as a teacher and writer. He currently teaches at Marmara University, Istanbul, as a professor of *tafsir*. His translation of the Qur'an is one of the most popular *tafsir*s ever published in Turkish.

- BAYRAM YENIKAYA holds a PhD on mathematics from the University of Minnesota. He represented Turkey national team at Canada International Math Olympiad, 1996, and won Silver Medal.

Knowledge and Responsibility

ISLAMIC PERSPECTIVES ON SCIENCE

Edited by
Ali Ünal

New Jersey

Published by Tughra Books
335 Clifton Avenue
Clifton, New Jersey, 07011, USA

www.tughrabooks.com

Library of Congress Cataloging-in-Publication Data

Islamic perspectives on science : knowledge and responsibility / edited
    by Ali Unal.
      p. cm.
    Originally published: Izmir : Kaynak, 1998.
    Includes bibliographical references and index.
    ISBN 1-59784-069-6 (pbk.)
    1. Islam and science.   I. Ünal, Ali.
  BP190.5.S3I856 2007
  297.2'65--dc22

                                                          2006031138

ISBN-13: 978-1-59784-069-9

Printed by
National Book Network

TABLE OF CONTENTS

Preface..vii

Islam and Science: An Overview / Abasi Kiyimba.............................1

Stating the problem...1
Identifying the issue 2
Science is no stranger to the Muslim world..4
Muslim scientists in history 7
The science–religion conflict: Reality or myth?..................................8
Science in the Qur'an 11
Muslims and problems posed by modern science 16
The viability of an Islamic science 21
A possible meeting point...23
Conclusion...25
Additional sources...27

Science and Religion / M. Fethullah Gülen & Ali Ünal......................28

The civilization that Islam created 28
Science and the modern scientific approach......................................32
Conflict between religion and science..36
Does the Qur'an contain everything? 41
The concept of science and technology...45
Two different fields for science and religion? 49
Cartesian dualism 49
Nature displays Divine Unity 52
What does the command Read! Signify? 56
Does the Qur'an allude to scientific developments? 58
Examples...61
Why we refer to science and scientific facts 73

Causality and the Qur'anic Worldview / Yamine Mermer................78

What a Falling Stone Means / Salih Adem 87

The Universe in the Light of Modern Physics / Salih Adem 93

Religion and Science: Shared Responsibilities / M. Saif Islam 99

    The goal of science 99
    Science without religion, religion without science 100
    Science and exploitation 103
    The Islamic approach to science 104
    "Believe in order to understand" 107
    A mentality of domination 110
    A united field theory 112
    References 113

Worldwide Corruption by Scientific Materialism / Suat Yildirim 114

Mathematics is Real: Why and How? / Bayram Yenikaya 119

    The language of numbers 119
    What flowers reveal 122

Notes 124
Index 133

PREFACE

This collection of essays seeks to provide some hope and meaning to the enterprise of modern science. Science has become disconnected from morality and religion, even from the general culture of our societies, despite the fact that our daily lives are so strongly influenced by the technology it enables. People generally feel that science has its own rules and momentum, perhaps even a will of its own, as if it were not the work of rational human beings who can choose what they study and how they apply their knowledge.

Consequently, alongside their wonder at scientific achievements and gratitude for the easier life that technology has made possible, people harbor a definite uneasiness about science and technology. For example, they fear that new methods of breeding animals and processing foods will produce, sooner or later, something inimical to human life, something that will generate terrible plagues and diseases. They worry that climate changes will affect the seasons and radically alter the life-cycles of innumerable tiny creatures, which will either die out or over-reproduce and thereby irrecoverably devastate a given region's ecological balance. They are afraid that somewhere some scientists, despite every legal prohibition, will clone human beings for profit, regardless of the incalculably negative consequences for the legal and moral relationships between parents and children, brothers and sisters, and for the psychological and emotional life that result from those relationships.

These and other fears are staple features of science-fiction books and movies, most of which confront humanity with a horrifying and terrifying future. But even greater than all of these fears is the general dread that science and technology are somehow unstoppable. Governments can appoint committees to discuss biomedical ethics and committees to impose fines for environmental degradation, and so on, but scientists will continue their projects. In addition, economic competition being what it is, the experiments and discoveries of science will continue to find their way into technology and our lives, whether for good or evil.

In essence, this general dread of science and technology is actually a fear of our unique power to understand and intervene in the natural world. It often appears that science and technology are autonomous, answerable only to their own processes, rules, and momentum. We wonder if they are being exercised responsibly, and ask questions like: Are they connected to moral authority? Can they be regulated by political authority? What are their particular purposes? Do the people behind science and technology do what they do because they can, regardless of whether we want them to do it or not? The principle seems to be that if it is possible it will get done, regardless of our objections or moral qualms. Perhaps, to borrow from ancient Greek mythology, we stole the knowledge and power that science and technology enable us to have, and, regarding ourselves as guilty thieves, are afraid of getting caught and being punished for what we have done. In other words, our general dread issues from a feeling of guilt.

Each one of us has been endowed with consciousness and with abilities to reflect and to speak. As a reflective being, we realize that we have a deep need for a moral dimension to our existence and an ultimate purpose for that existence. Cloning people horrifies most of us because it makes death meaningless. If each of us can be replicated, our "life" will never end. Without an end, there can be no ultimate purpose, conclusion, or escape. The real possibility of eternal life on this Earth suddenly makes us realize that we do not really want it. What we really want is to understand and achieve meaningfulness in our lives.

The traditional religious view is that a limited and transient period of life on Earth is a blessing, and that death is the gateway to possible perfection in another mode of life, a perfection that is both impossible and inconceivable in this world. If we close that gateway, we shut ourselves off from that hope of perfectibility and shut ourselves in permanently with all the confusion, imperfection, cruelty, injustice, failure, and disappointment of our present lives.

The enterprise of modern science—its rules, processes, and technological promises—only appears to be a global phenomenon. It is perhaps the most important and powerful part of modern Western culture. It appears to be global because for almost three centuries Western civilization has exercised an unprecedented degree of military and economic dominance over all other societies, cultures, and civilizations. During this period, Western civilization has been distancing itself from its own religious and moral traditions and moving toward the illusion of an ever-greater degree of freedom for an individual to choose whatever intellectual or moral authority is most pleasing.

In the most advanced Western societies, as well as those sections of non-Western societies that have accepted and imitated the West successfully, institutionalized religion has survived by compromising with that trend. Following this path, however, has made religion even narrower, more personal and private, until practically its only public function is to maintain some vestige of a link with the past, a trace of a collective national or cultural identity.

It is a matter of principle that scientific inquiry must owe nothing to the guidance of religious authority, past or present, or make any assumptions other than the minimum methodological assumptions necessary to conduct a disciplined inquiry. Above all, science must make no assumptions about the ultimate origin or purpose of the phenomena into which it inquires, for its sole task is to find out how things operate and how the operation of one thing affects the operation of another. It is not surprising that the most consistent fruit of such inquiry is technological power, for understanding and mastering how certain effects are caused gives us a mechanical advantage over them. This advantage then allows us to calculate and manipulate enough of the processes involved for any short-term gains wherever and whenever we want them.

Yet despite modern Western civilization's failure to improve significantly our well-being in any domain other than that of our physical and material life, people generally believe that there is no alternative. Either we accept the Western way of pursuing science and the modes of thinking and living that go with it, or we avoid it. If we choose the latter, we condemn ourselves to a narrow, primitive mode of life that does not enter into commercial and cultural relations with other societies, which means that our own intellectual and cultural life loses its dynamism and becomes stagnant.

NOTE: All footnotes identifying people or explaining concepts are taken from www.britannica.com, unless otherwise indicated.

ISLAM AND SCIENCE: AN OVERVIEW

Abasi Kiyimba

STATING THE PROBLEM

The relationship between Islam and science has been the focal point of scholarly exertion and controversy for quite a long period of time. In 1983, Jameelah lashed out at modern science:

> Modern science is guided by no moral value but naked materialism and arrogance. The whole branch of knowledge and its applications is contaminated by the same evil. Science and technology are totally dependent upon the set of ideals and values cherished by its members. If the roots of a tree are rotten, then the tree is rotten; therefore all its fruits are rotten.[1]

Nearly 700 years earlier, the renowned Muslim scholar Imam al-Ghazali[2] had expressed fears that the clarity and precision of mathematical demonstrations could lead those who studied them (superficially) to deny God's Attributes. His objection was not to mathematics as such, but to its possible repercussions, as seen in the following quote:

> Even if geometry and arithmetic do not contain notions that are harmful to religious belief, we nevertheless fear that one may be attracted through them to doctrines that are dangerous.[3]

Similar views have been expressed by various scholars, each according to their convictions and the time in which they lived. But, as one would expect, there is no consensus among Muslim scholars on this subject. Jamal al-Din al-Afghani[4] said bluntly:

Those who forbid science and knowledge in the belief that they are safeguarding the Islamic religion are really the enemies of that religion. The Islamic religion is the closest of religions to science and knowledge and there is no incompatibility between science and knowledge and the foundation of the Islamic religion.[5]

Seyed Ahmad Khan,[6] a Muslim scholar who expressed a similar position, albeit more mildly, stated that science is the work of God that scientists occasionally were honored to understand:

I am fully convinced that the Work of God and the Word of God can never be antagonistic to each other; we may through the fault of our knowledge sometimes make mistakes in understanding the meaning of the Word.[7]

In our own time, Sardar has asserted a view that enjoys considerable popularity among contemporary Muslim scholars and opinion leaders:

While science itself is neutral, it is the attitude by which we approach science that makes it secular or Islamic. The Islamic approach recognizes the limitations of the human mind and reason, and acknowledges that all knowledge is the property of God.[8]

These and similar views show that Muslim scholars do not agree on which approach Islam should take toward modern science. The debate recently has shifted from rejecting scientific discoveries as "dangerous" to searching for the most appropriate way of coexisting with modern science. Views have ranged from a total acceptance of Western methods and paradigms to a total rejection of them, and calls for devising an alternative Islamic science. This debate has attracted both Muslim and non-Muslim scholars.

IDENTIFYING THE ISSUE

In this article, I discuss how Islam approaches modern science and present some background to the debate as it now stands. Such background issues may come up for mention, reference, and discussion. In addition, as our understanding of *Islam* and *science* changes with time and place, I will define them below.

Islam is a belief and way of life that attributes all power and order to the Supreme Being, God, Who created everything and tells us to worship Him alone. He guides humanity through His Books, the Qur'an, and His Messengers and Prophets, of whom Prophet Muhammad is the last.[9] Islam offers humanity success in this world and the next, which entails peace and well-being between each person and God, and between each person and his or her neighbor. It tells us to make the most of whatever benefits creation contains, while simultaneously being aware of our spiritual destiny. Islam therefore provides a complete code of guidance in moral, social, political, economic, and a wide range of other issues.

Science is a body of knowledge that we acquire through observation and analysis. The term is quite broad, for almost every branch of human inquiry can be called a science. Given this, we can talk about *religious* and *social* sciences. In this paper, I use *science* to mean the physical sciences, whether theoretical or applied, that use consistent experimentation, observation, and inference in an attempt to comprehend the physical and material universe. The relationship between such science and Islam is the core issue of this debate.

The present state of science in the Muslim world has been a focal point in some of these discussions. In some cases, such scholars as Hoodbhoy reach rather unjust conclusions about Islam and science.[10] To set the record straight, we should remind ourselves that the state of science in the Muslim world today does not reflect the elevated position that Islam gives to science and other forms of knowledge. In the past, Muslim leaders treated scientific research as a priority and provided encouragement and facilities to scientists, with the result that science prospered in Muslim lands. Thus this period of scientific prosperity is a necessary part of the background to this discussion.

SCIENCE IS NO STRANGER TO THE MUSLIM WORLD

Modern science is sometimes presented as a stranger to whom Islam has to adapt or for whom a place has to be found in Islam as a necessity dictated by the changing times. It is therefore necessary to make the point that Islamic history records abundant scientific exertions by Muslim scientists who also were outstanding Muslim theologians and philosophers. Ghiles notes that:

> At its peak about one thousand years ago, the Muslim world made a remarkable contribution to science, notably mathematics and medicine. Baghdad in its heyday and southern Spain built universities to which thousands flocked. Rulers surrounded themselves with scientists and artists.[11]

This tribute is one of many that Western scholars are belatedly paying to Muslim civilization. Sarton records that :

> From the second half of the eighth to the end of the eleventh century, Arabic was the scientific, the progressive language of mankind ... anyone wishing to be well-informed, up-to-date, had to study Arabic ...[12]

He then gives a lengthy list of Muslim scientists who bore the torch of civilization while, in Hoodbhoy's words, "Europeans were preoccupied with disembowelling heretics."[13] Citing the work of a Muslim scientist, Sarton writes the following about Robert of Chester's translation of al-Khwarizmi's[14] work: "The importance of this particular translation can hardly be exaggerated. It may be said to mark the beginning of European Algebra."[15]

Gandz is even more elaborate in explaining modern science's debt to Islamic civilization:

> Al-Khwarizmi's algebra is regarded as the foundation and cornerstone of the sciences. In a sense, al-Khwarizmi is more entitled to be called "the father of algebra" than Diophantus because al-Khwarizmi was the first to teach algebra in an elementary form and for its own sake, [whereas] Diophantus is primarily concerned with the theory of numbers.[16]

Rosenthal presses the same point when he writes:

> Muslim science and medicine are important as part of the conti-
> nuity of the classical tradition in the East as well as the West which
> was greatly indebted to Muslim civilization in these fields.[17]

Professor de Santillana of the Massachusetts Institute of
Technology says of al-Biruni[18]:

> In al-Biruni, the greatest scientist of Islam, we meet a mind in
> no way different from the Western lay scientific mind at its best.
> His religious faith is secure but ... does not impede his freedom
> of judgement, his love of fact, his free-wheeling curiosity, his easy
> sarcasm, his strict and watchful cult of intellectual integrity.[19]

Hoodbhoy, while quite critical of *Islamic* science, has good
words for the scientists of the Golden Age of Muslim civilization:

> Today we remember Nasir al-Din al-Tusi [1201-1274] for his
> trigonometry, 'Umar Khayyam for his solution of cubic equa-
> tions, Jabir ibn Hayyan [8/9th c.] for the ingenuity of his chem-
> ical apparatus, al-Jazari [12th c.] for his intricate machines ...[20]

The invention of the zero by Muslim mathematicians is one
of the most spectacular contributions of Islamic civilization to
modern science. It is difficult to imagine modern mathematics
without it. In reference to this contribution, al-Daffa notes that:

> The zero's creation opened the way for the entire concept of
> algebraic positive and negative numbers, which are used for cal-
> culations, identification of electric charge and discharge, for nav-
> igation etc.[21]

Of course Muslim scientists were preceded by others,
notably those of the prior Greek and Roman civilizations. Far
from shunning them as irrelevant, Muslims studied their work
and acknowledged benefiting from the work of Euclid (flourished about 300 BCE), Archimedes (d. 211 BCE), Apollonios (b.
212 BCE), Pythagoras (d. c. 497 BCE), Ephesus, Vitruvius, Pergamos, Ptolemy, and others. For them, science was an honest dis-

cipline of experiment and observation. One scientist, Abu al-Faraj 'Abdullah Tayyib (d. 1043) states:

> In our studies we have followed in the footsteps of our prede-
> cessors and taken pains to understand their works well. We
> have also discovered, in connection with obscure statements and
> explanations of theirs, a number of ideas going beyond what
> they have said.

Early Muslim scientists worked in an atmosphere of bor-
rowing, acknowledging, and innovating. Modern science, so much
of which is attributed to the West, borrowed from scientists who
lived in the Islamic world (not all of whom were Muslim), although
they are rarely acknowledged. Al-Hassan and Hill report that al-
Muradi, an eleventh-century Muslim scientist, borrowed technology from elsewhere (including northern Europe) to redesign
the famous Arab water-clock.[22] Later, his clocks spread throughout Europe and can still be seen in those European areas that
value antiquity.

Clearly, there has been a great deal of scientific interdepend-
ence between Muslim civilization and the current home of modern science: Western civilization. However we describe *modern
science*, Muslim scientists had a major historical role in shaping
it, for as Hoodbhoy says:

> [Science] is like a building always in use but in perpetual repair,
> continuously growing in size and adding to itself new exten-
> sions and sections ... [and] individual scientists, like a toiling
> worker ant, are but minions who help in the creation of this
> giant repository of human knowledge.[23]

Muslims should see this statement in the context of Sardar's
observation that all knowledge is God's property. The Muslim
world contributed through the scientists it produced. We also
should note that these Muslim scientists prospered partly because
of the interest and support of that era's leaders. The success of
the officially favored Banu Musa brothers of Baghdad is a good
example. Al-Hassan and Hill report of Caliph al-Mu'taqid (d. 902),

that: "Caliph Mu'taqid, for example, provided in his palace lodgings and rooms for all branches of sciences, and professors were paid salaries for teaching there."[24]

MUSLIM SCIENTISTS IN HISTORY

Al-Hassan and Hill, Sarton, Nasr, and others give long but by no means exhaustive lists of Muslim scientists and their achievements. Certain scientists have been too imposing to be ignored, if only because they have dictated trends in modern science. Among them are al-Khwarizmi, whose original studies in algebra provided a stepping stone for modern mathematics. Abu al-Fath 'Umar ibn Ibrahim al-Khayyami (Omar Khayyam, 1038/48-1123/24) is celebrated almost to the same degree. Thabit ibn Qurra (c. 836-901), a Sabian[25] from Harran, is remembered for his authoritative work on mathematics, physics, medicine, and astronomy.

Maslama al-Majriti (d. c. 1007), an authority on alchemy and author of *The Sage's Step* and *The Aim of the Wise*, was also a distinguished astronomer and mathematician. Nasir al-Din al-Tusi (1201-74), ranked by some as the greatest Muslim scientist after Ibn Sina (Avicenna, 980-1037), was a great historian, astronomer, and mathematician. Mahmud ibn Mas'ud Qutb al-Din al-Shirazi (d. 1311) excelled in mathematics and astronomy. Of no less significance are al-Jazari (12th c.) author of *The Compendium of the Theory and Practice of Mechanical Arts*, and ninth-century Baghdad's Banu Musa brothers, who enjoyed access to the Bayt al-Hikmah. Their book, *The Book of Ingenious Devices*, had a great influence on later mathematical and engineering studies.[26]

In medicine, Ibn Sina is legendary even in the West. His *Canon of Medicine* and *The Book of Healing* were long-term staples for university academics, especially in France. Muhammad ibn Zakariyya al-Razi (Rhazes, 865-925) is remembered for his *The Secret of Secrets* and for his outstanding medical treatise *The Treatise on Smallpox and Measles*. Abu 'Ali al-Hassan ibn al-Haytham (Alhazen, c. 965-c. 1039) was a great physicist whose *Book on Optics* earned him a place in scientific history. Ibn Rushd (Averroes,

d. 1198) studied both science and philosophy and made invaluable commentaries on Aristotle's works. Al-Biruni (973-1050), described by de Santillana as the greatest Muslim scientist, is respected both in the East and the West for his commitment and consistency in the search for knowledge. He is the author of *Chronology of Ancient Nations* and many other works.

Other great scientists of note were the Christian philosopher–scientist Hunayn ibn Ishaq (d. 809-73), who wrote *Aphorisms of the Philosophers*; Abu Yusuf Ya'qub ibn Ishaq al-Kindi (c. 801-c. 873), a philosopher–scientist; Jabir ibn Hayyan (flourished around 776), a great polymath with numerous publications to his name, especially in chemistry; the philosopher Abu Nasr al-Farabi (Alfarabius, d. 950); Abu al-Hassan al-Mas'udi (d. 957), a geographer and geologist; and Baha' al-Din al-'Amili (d. 1621), a philosopher, theologian, mathematician, and architect.

Many more names could be added. The few names given here are to remind readers that classical Muslim and non-Muslim scholars in the Islamic world had no dogmatic interest in science; rather, they sought scientific knowledge, and their findings helped lay the foundation for modern science. One aspect of their lives that could benefit contemporary Muslim scientists is that these scholars were simultaneously scientists and devout religious scholars who pursued both paths without seeing any contradiction in so doing.

THE SCIENCE–RELIGION CONFLICT: REALITY OR MYTH?

Islam promotes humanity's material as well as spiritual well-being. Since Islam enjoins its followers to seek and utilize knowledge to better their lives here and in the Hereafter, Muslims must study science, if only to protect Islamic civilization's political and social structures. Prophet Muhammad fought to protect Islam using the weapons of the day. This means that those Muslims strove for technological equality, if not superiority, with their contemporaries. Sardar writes:

Science is the basic problem-solving tool of any civilization. Without science a civilization cannot maintain its political and social structures or meet the basic needs of its people and culture. In short, science is the tool which ultimately moulds a civilization: it is a physical expression of its worldview.[27]

Many respected scholars have tackled the relationship between Islam and science and have made it clear that, in principle, Islam has no conflict with science. We also have noted Sardar's assertion that all knowledge, including scientific knowledge, is the property of God. This assertion is accepted by all contemporary Muslim scholars. The big question now is whether modern science is acceptable as it is, if it should be applied Islamically, or if Muslims should abandon any direct relationship with modern science and develop *Islamic* science.

In the past, Muslim scholars of particular persuasions sometimes criticized science as ungodly and immoral, persecuted scientists, and rejected their innovations and inventions as dangerous to belief. This is one of the reasons why science declined in Muslim lands. For example, al-Kindi, the great scientist and favorite at Caliph Ma'mun's court, had to flee for his life when al-Mutawwakil assumed power. He died a quiet and depressed man. Ibn Khaldun (1332-1406), one of the great Muslim thinkers of the later period and famous for his contribution to the study of embryonic sciences, was ostracized by the more conservative 'ulama' of his time for being too "rationalistic" in his methods of inquiry.[28] Such occurrences were unfortunate, but we can regret them without prejudicing Islam's essential attitude toward science, and should not let them blind us to some Muslim scholars' legitimate objections to various modern scientific methods and applications.

How has the Christian Church traditionally looked at science and its practitioners? We must answer this question because it is mainly Christo-centric scholars who have tried to sully Islam's reputation with the most negative portrayals while keeping a loud silence about the appalling record of Christianity on this matter.

For over 1,000 years, the Church forbade Christians to believe that people lived on the other side of the planet. This belief originated with St. Augustine.[29] Earth was believed to be flat, and if there were people on the other side they were definitely standing upside down, an idea that the Church found unacceptable. Similarly, on the authority of St. Paul,[30] Christians were required to believe that disease, famine, pestilence, and air pollution were caused by demons. Thus vaccination was forbidden at a time when such Muslim scientists as al-Razi were conducting research in this field. Lightning and thunderbolts were believed to result from the five sins of impertinence, incredulity, neglect of Church repairs, fraud in paying tithes to clergy, and oppressing surbordinates. While such great Muslim scientists as al-Majriti, al-Shirazi, and al-Mas'udi were writing at length on astronomy, geography, and geology, Christians were forbidden to study cosmic bodies and geology. As recently as 1850, Pope Pius IX forbade Italy's scientific congress to meet in Bologna because geology was on the program. Dr. Boylston's work on smallpox vaccines, Benjamin Franklin's lightning rods, and Immanuel Kant's theory of nebula and the stars all were met with great displeasure and resistance by the Church.

When Copernicus[31] published his *Commentariolus* in 1514, he was encouraged by Pope Clement VII to develop it into what later became *De Revolutionibus Orbium Coelestium* (On the Revolutions of the Heavenly Spheres), published in 1543. This work overthrew Ptolemy's geocentric astronomy and replaced it with the heliocentric model. By 1616, however, Copernicus' views and the entire "Copernican revolution" were judged dangerous because they contradicted the Church's views on the cosmos. Copernicus, himself a churchman, a canonicus of the Cathedral of Frauenburg (Poland), and a doctor of canon law, was condemned as a heretic and excommunicated (23 February 1616), long after his death.

Although his views were criminalized by the Church, they continued to spread and served as a foundation upon which Galileo, Kepler, Huygens, and Newton built their research. Galileo has become legendary for his confrontation with the Church, the more significantly so because he was a devout Christian. Pope Urban VIII, who condemned him to life imprisonment, was his former friend and protector Cardinal Maffe Barberni. Perhaps this gave Galileo a false sense of security. Later scientific studies vindicated Galileo, but the Church maintained an unrepentant (but probably embarrassed) silence. Some historians have tried to blame Galileo for this conflict, as seen in the following quote:

> A talented publicist, he [Galileo] helped to popularize the pursuit of science. However, his quarrelsome nature led him into an unfortunate controversy with the Church.[32]

It has long been known that Galileo was right and that the Church authorities were wrong. It may well be that Galileo's enemies among the university establishment (Aristotelians or Neo-Platonists) exploited his talent for controversy and maneuvred him into a battle with the Church. But that does not make the Church's response his fault. It is rather depressing that it took the Vatican over 350 years to issue a formal retraction of its position. On 9 May 1983, Pope John Paul II made a statement that came close to an apology:

> The Church's experience in the Galileo affair and after it has led to a more mature attitude ... It is only by humble and assiduous study that (the Church) learns to dissociate the essentials of the faith from the scientific system of a given age.[33]

Islam, however, does not "dissociate" scientific systems from belief's essentials, for science is belief's practical department. If it is handled responsibly and guided correctly, it can be a great help in fulfilling Islam's mission.

SCIENCE IN THE QUR'AN

The Qur'an is a book of guidance that contains a universal and all-embracing message for humanity, regardless of time and place. As it covers every aspect of life, it would be surprising if it did not contain science. A thorough study of the Qur'an reveals the roots of many scientific discoveries that have been or will be made, even though Muslim scholars may not be in a position to talk authoritatively about such things without making specific studies of them.

The Qur'an offers hints that could lead to major discoveries if followed up diligently. This is why earlier generations of Muslim scholars, who combined Qur'anic knowledge with scientific curiosity and competence, excelled. Contemporary scholars have analyzed Qur'anic references to various scientific subjects and have produced major texts in astronomy, embryonic biology, the movement of bees, mountains, Earth's composition, plants, and many other subjects. Even those who wish to deny the presence of science in the Qur'an have to admit defeat when studying such verses as 96:1-5 (embryology) and 36:36-40, 91:1-4, 21:30, 55:7, 79:28, and many others (cosmology). These hints give useful insights to researchers as well as blessings and encouragement to Muslims to engage in science. If pursued intelligently and without bias, such hints can lead to startling discoveries and inventions.

However, there is a whole tradition of scholars who have tried to read science into and out of the Qur'an as an end in itself. They "find" almost every scientific invention and discovery in the Qur'an and provide a scientific rationalization for each Qur'anic prescription or prohibition. Some of this work has been useful, for it has reawakened Muslims to the value of their inheritance and should rekindle the desire for further research now that they understand that the Qur'an supports such undertakings. But in many cases, such scholars either have overstepped the limits and exposed Islam to Western ridicule or have nourished many Muslims' inferiority complexes by requiring that the Qur'an's status as a Divine Revelation must be "proved" by science.

In 1961, the Egyptian scientist El-Fandy published his *On Cosmic Verses in the Qur'an,* in which he described the Qur'an as "the best example of scientific expression."[34] To illustrate this assertion, he explained some verses in terms of modern astronomical discoveries and scientific theories, among them the "Big Bang" theory. The Muslim world cheered him; Western scientists smiled patronizingly, satisfied that Muslims could not have much to offer if they needed Western science to prove the Qur'an's accuracy.

But the trend had only just started. Azizul-Hassan Abbasi, a Pakistani neuropsychiatrist, asserted in *The Qur'an and Mental Hygiene* that he had found Qur'an-based cures for diabetes, tuberculosis, stomach ulcers, rheumatism, arthritis, high blood pressure, asthma, dysentery, and paralysis.[35] In the end, the claims turned out to be mere intellectual amusement, for he did not follow them up in the hope of offering the world any medical breakthroughs and triumphs for Islam.

In 1976, French surgeon Maurice Bucaille published *The Bible, the Qur'an and Science* and sparked a wave of excitement in the Muslim world. He followed it up in 1989 with a pamphlet entitled "The Qur'an and Science." *The Bible, the Qur'an and Science* has been reprinted several times and translated into various Muslim languages. After subjecting both the Bible and the Qur'an to rigorous tests against the findings of modern science in geology, astronomy, animal and plant sciences, and human reproduction, he concluded that:

> The Qur'an most definitely did not contain a single proposition at variance with the most firmly established modern knowledge; modern man's findings concerning the absence of scientific error are therefore in complete agreement with the Muslim exegete's conception of the Qur'an as a book of Revelation.[36]

Muslims were excited, for their Book had been "proved" correct. Bucaille's sweeping suggestion that modern findings concerning "the absence of error" was endorsed by the Qur'an was missed by an excited Muslim community. The marriage between the Qur'an and modern scientific findings was a completely happy one, and no one could commit error. His conclusion that "it is impossible not to admit the existence of scientific errors in the

Bible" also was swallowed wholesale by the Muslims, and one dissented at the risk of going against the majority tide.

Muslims always had taken on faith that the Qur'an contains no errors because it is the Word of God, while the Bible (in its present form) is not a true revelation from God. But now they had *scientific* proof! The rules of the game changed. Modern science was accepted by a cross-section of Muslims as the umpire between the Qur'an and the Bible. Bucaille became a hero to some Muslims. At conferences to which he was not invited, many people, even highly learned Muslim scholars, quoted him at great length. At other conferences, more of Bucaille than faith per se was discussed in relation to the Qur'an's authenticity. The time bomb that Bucaille had set could be detonated by the wilful search for scientific error in the Qur'an or something to prove the Bible's scientific accuracy.

In April 1985, the *Bulletin of the Islamic Medical Association of South Africa* published an article entitled "Canadian Scholar Confirms Qur'an and Hadith on Human Embryology." Bucaille notwithstanding, it was still big news in the Muslim community that scientist Keith Moore, chairman of the Anatomy Department of the University of Toronto's School of Medicine, had "discovered" the agreement between Islam and the contemporary understanding of embryology. Moore, like Bucaille, became a favorite of Muslim conference organizers—presumably to help "confirm" further that the Qur'an and Hadith[37] were scientifically correct.

Shamsul Haq, like El-Fandy before him, produced Qur'anic "evidence" in support of the "Big Bang" theory after pouncing on the "seeds of the theory of relativity and quantum mechanics in the Qur'an."[38] Khuda provides Qur'anic evidence for the theory of the biosphere's development.[39] Rahman presents the Qur'an as a textbook of science.[40] In this 332-page volume, he covers 27 subjects and says that the Qur'an covers even more. It is notable that, like others before him, his "discoveries" in the Qur'an already were made by modern science.

There have been other attempts to reciprocally "legitimize" the Qur'an and modern science. As noted earlier, some of this work has been useful and other work has gone too far and resulted in absurdity. Bashiruddin Mahmood, a Pakistani nuclear engineer, is quoted as suggesting that the jinn, whom God made out of fire, should be used as a source of energy to combat the energy crisis. Such outstanding theologians as Abu Ishaq al-Shabati have been irked by these searches for science in the Qur'an. Sayyid Qutb, describing the whole exercise as "a methodological error," has insisted that while the Qur'an contains guidance on scientific subjects, it is not a textbook of science.[41]

Even after such "findings," Muslims were not prepared for Egyptian engineer Khalifa's adventurous experimentation using the computer to ascertain and assert the Qur'an's accuracy. Obsessed with the Qur'an's mathematical nature, he contrived the "theory of 19" as the miraculous number around which the Qur'an was constructed.[42]

He argued as follows: The first verse of the Qur'an (*Bismillah, al-Rahman, al-Rahim*) has 19 letters. When the 28 letters of the Arabic alphabet are assigned certain numerical values, and when 19 is written corresponding to its alphabet, it spells *wahid* (one of God's Names). The Qur'an has 114 chapters, a multiple of 19; the first Qur'anic revelation (96:1-5) consists of 19 words and has 76 letters, another multiple of 19; and so on. Khalifa's detailed numerological analysis of the Qur'an excited many Muslims who saw it as a new way to "authenticate" the Qur'an. He was quoted at international and local conferences, and was a special favorite at Muslim student seminars. Even the renowned Muslim preacher Ahmad Deedat used his findings, for example, in his undated pamphlet "Al-Qur'an: The Ultimate Miracle."

Later Khalifa was to shock even his admirers when he declared that he had calculated the exact Day of Judgment,[43] and that his theory of 19 had revealed errors in the last two verses of *Surat al-Tawba*.[44] More shocking still was his claim:

> This marks the advent of a new era in religion; an era where faith is no longer needed. There is no need to "believe" when one "knows." People of the past generation were required to believe in God, and uphold His commandments on faith. With the advent of the physical evidence reported in this book, we no longer believe that God exists; we know that God exists.[45]

In other words, scientific "evidence" has made Islam's pillars of belief obsolete. Now, if we want to believe in any truth at all, we need "evidence" (and *scientific* evidence at that), for this new era has no room for (religious) belief. But this was not all from Khalifa. He decided that since we had scientific evidence and means, even Prophet Muhammad had no further role to play in Islam, for when we seek *religious* instruction from the Prophet or any source other than God, we support Satan's claim that God needs a partner.[46]

Incredible as it may sound, some Muslims followed Khalifa even on this point. Kassim Ahmad, his disciple in Malaysia, wrote a pamphlet denouncing Hadith. This version of the experiment with science and the Qur'an had gone that far![47] Khalifa then equated the mission of a scientist in this scientific age to that of a Prophet and actually described himself as a Prophet.[48] There is no doubt that Imam al-Ghazali, if were still alive, would have felt vindicated in rejecting mathematics for its potential danger to belief. Khalifa's scientific misadventures give us a good example of the way modern science can be abused by those claiming to champion the cause of Islam, and of the way the Qur'an can be abused by those purporting to validate it.

MUSLIMS AND PROBLEMS POSED BY MODERN SCIENCE

With every passing day, modern science advances another step. Some of its steps bewilder Muslims. For example, what are they to make of sperm clinics that enable a woman to have a child without a known father, or of attempts to grow organs for transplantation into people by injecting pigs with human genes? Some of these technological innovations are directly antagonistic to Islam's doctrine and spirit. Further, there is the problem of modern scientists' failure to appreciate their limitations in matters of knowledge and their attempt to make their unbelief in God a virtue. The problem between Islam and modern science will continue to exist until modern scientists accept human limitations. Soliman summarizes this point admirably:

> Since science is still unable to account for the Prophets' miracles which are historically true and can in no way be discredited ... we can judge that science with all its very many triumphs is still a dwarf. We can also safely conclude that there are heavenly ideas which man cannot comprehend however much he strives to do so, and that his ability to learn has a limit. It is therefore strange that there should be such a conflict in our two sources of knowledge.[49]

Despite this contemporary Muslim scholar's very conciliatory approach, today's leading scientific researchers are not about the Muslims' to accept this and similar calls for a ceasefire. This reveals that disagreement is not really with science per se, but with those who misapply it and insist upon its inherent secular (and atheistic) nature, as does, for example, Hoodbhoy:

> Whether one likes it or not, it is indisputably true that modern science is completely secular in character. There is no appeal to divine authority for verification of scientific facts; the existence of such authority is neither affirmed nor denied ... experiment and logical consistency are the sole arbiters of truth—of no consequence is the scientist's mood or moral character.[50]

But that is not all that Hoodbhoy has to say. He is irritated that "religious dogmatists of all persuasions have long excoriated science as a godless pursuit destructive of divinely inspired morality."

This confident rejection of divinity and morality is what really accounts for the Muslims' discomfort and bewilderment in their relationship with modern science. Muslims believe that the absolute truth originates from God, to Whom they pray at least five times a day and to Whom they turn whenever they are baffled or tormented by any phenomenon. But modern scientists even frown upon prayer, much to the dismay of Muslims. J. W. N. Sullivan thinks it is absurd for anyone to pray for rain, saying that:

> The belief that nature is orderly is not yet universal ... we still find congregations praying for rain, although they would hesitate, probably, to pray that the sun might stand still. That is because astronomy is a more developed science than meteorology.[51]

In other words, Muslims will stop praying for rain when they learn more about meteorology. Such views repel Muslims. After observing the order in nature, scientists do not take the next logical step of wondering who established such an order. Little wonder therefore that they constantly irritate such leading Muslim scholars as Abu A'la al-Mawdudi.

But others have not been content with Sullivan's gentle mockery. Renan[52] denounced Islam for stifling science by failing to distinguish between *spiritual* and *temporal*. He then described its "dogma" as "the heaviest chain that humanity has ever borne."[53] Renan, a learned man aware of the historical battles between scientists and the Church, ignored them in his attack on Islam. In other words, the Muslims' problem with modern science is not just the rejection of God or the too-often immoral applications of science, but also with those scientists who ridicule and defame Islam possibly out of commitment to rival religions [or to no religion at all].

Rejecting God necessarily leads to further complications, notably how to account for the origin and essence of humanity and matter. Scientists have numerous contradictory theories for this purpose, which makes the whole undertaking capricious and vague and thus gives Muslims a reason to feel a sense of triumph in their insistence on Divinity.

Darwin's[54] theory of evolution constitutes the most traumatic clash between Islam and science. The Qur'an says:

> Surely We have created man of the best stature as the perfect pattern of creation. Then we have reduced him to the lowest of the low except those who believe and do good, righteous deeds; so there is for them a reward constant and beyond measure. (95:4-6)

By contrast, Darwin says:

> When I view all beings not as special creations, but as lineal descendants of some few beings ... they seem to me to become enabled.[55]

Even in the West, Darwin's theory of evolution was received with great misgivings. Many people not known for their (Christian) piety were alarmed at the idea of being descended from lower animals. One interesting spontaneous reaction to Darwin's theory was:

> The wife the Bishop of Worcester, when informed about Darwin's theory, commented, "Descended from apes! My dear, let us hope that it is not true, but if it is, let us hope that it may not become generally known."[56]

She was reacting instinctively to offended dignity. The Qur'an states that humanity was created in the best pattern, and is reduced by God to the lowest of the low when humanity makes itself unworthy of this pattern. But Darwin and others like him want to assert that humanity evolved from lower beings. From the Muslim viewpoint, this denies God's role as Creator and lowers humanity's dignity.

The problem with modern science is that sometimes the observations made may not be sufficient to prove a hypothesis, even though this lack of sufficient information may lead people to accept it as sound. Islam has no problem with a systematic search for knowledge that does not involve doctrinal and moral trespass. But those scholars whom Sardar has termed *Bucaillist* would have a problem. They would use a scientific finding to examine and interpret the Qur'an, develop a very impressive theory, and then have to abandon it when the underlying scientific finding [or theory] is disproven. We saw a similar development when Copernicus overthrew Ptolemy's views on astronomy after they had prevailed for 14 centuries. If any scholar had used Ptolemic cosmology (which was "modern" knowledge before the sixteenth century) to "prove" the Qur'an, the results would have been significantly different from what they would be today.

Using the same line of argument, we can predict that scholars who suggest that pork was forbidden because pigs have dangerous worms that are not easily killed by heat will have problems in the future. Scientists may develop breeding methods that overcome this problem. But since Muslims follow the Qur'an and science, pork will remain forbidden to them.

Scientific research is only an attempt to understand our world. No doubt it is a very useful attempt, but certainly not one in which, as Hoodbhoy would have us believe, inference and observation give science an "awesome power and authority."[57] This and similar attitudes of the modern world's worship of science have made scientific achievement an end in itself, and have left humanity racing recklessly toward self-destruction. People are haunted by Nagasaki and Hiroshima, bedevilled by endless conflict, and awaiting a nuclear or environmental disaster.

Islam does not consider the search for knowledge as a purposeless pursuit or an end in itself. Rather, it is a doctrinally and morally focused activity that should make people better inhabitants of this planet, worthier of the purpose for which they were created. Modern science is led, guided, and programmed by people who do not subscribe to the Islamic ideals of human purpose and dignity, and indeed flout them without a second thought. The question then arises: Does this make modern science a totally "rotten" activity that Muslims should shun, or is there another way?

THE VIABILITY OF AN ISLAMIC SCIENCE

Muslims have produced many responses to the excesses of modern science. Scholars of the Bucaille tradition, more than anything else, responded to accusations that Islam as a religion was false and anti-science. They revived the psychological confidence of the less-sure Muslims. But if Muslims were alone on the globe, these researchers would have achieved nothing as regards the accumulation of scientific knowledge that leads to building factories, cars, airplanes, computers, medical laboratories, and other facilities that make life easier. In other words, their "victories" were won in the psychological area and remained largely theoretical exercises. In the meantime, they continued to enjoy the results of modern science's advances.

Another group of scholars posited the idea of an Islamic science based on the following rationale: Modern science had failed to minister to humanity's needs beyond the surrounding psychophysical and natural worlds. As far back as 1968, Nasr published a full-length work entitled *Science and Civilization in Islam*, in which he gives biographical information about historical Muslim scientists, describes their contributions to the development of science, and offers a philosophical framework within which science in Islam should be conceived. He has followed this publication with several others, the most significant of which are: *The Encounter of Man and Nature: The Spiritual Crisis of Modern Man* (1968), *Islamic Science: An Illustrated Study* (1976), *An Introduction to Islamic Cosmological Doctrines* (1978), *Traditional Islam in the Modern World* (1987), and *The Need for a Sacred Science* (1993).

In all these works, he is concerned that humanity's spiritual essence is threatened by rapid and doctrineless industrialization, which is also a menace to natural order. He sums up his concern in the following words:

> Today more and more people are becoming aware that the applications of modern science ... have caused directly or indi-

rectly unprecedented environmental disasters, bringing about the real possibility of the total collapse of the natural order.[58]

Nasr's arguments are persuasive, and his works are good historical, philosophical, and even spiritual experiences that leave one wiser on Qur'anic symbolism in the Gnostic tradition. However, he is too theoretical and leaves the practical questions unanswered. After noting the metaphysical aspects of Islamic science that Nasr emphasizes, how are Muslims to relate to the modern science that is already in place? Can they really discard it and start all over again all on their own?

Sardar also favors developing an Islamic science that recognizes God's ownership over all knowledge. He has written several books on this, the most significant of which are: *The Future of Muslim Civilizations* (1987), *Islamic Futures: The Shape of Ideas to Come* (1988), and *Explorations in Islamic Science* (1989). It is clear from his work that proponents of Islamic science do not even agree on the definition. Sardar frowns at Nasr's Gnosticism, rejects *Bucaillism*, objects to Khalifa's nonsensical numerology, and accuses al-Faruqi of seeking to subordinate Islam to existing forms of knowledge by "Islamizing" it. For, according to Sardar, existing knowledge should fit into Islam instead of Islam fitting into existing knowledge.

Sardar argues that a civilization must have a scientific philosophy to survive. If it does not, it will have to adopt non-indigenous philosophies and all of their underlying assumptions. He proposes a framework within which scientific knowledge should be conceived in Islam. Although his ideas are much more in touch with reality than Nasr's Gnosticism, the fundamental problem remains: How can Muslims survive in the present world if they start again and go it alone while having to compete with modern science's technological grandeur in order to maintain Islamic civilization? Sardar's work is definitely substantive, but his achievement remains scholarly as distinct from practically scientific.

An Islamic science, one that is completely independent of modern science, may be an option for the future if those scientists involved in it can develop it practically and show how it can be used to solve practical problems. But today's question for Muslims is twofold: What is the best way to progress in a world dominated by modern science without transgressing Islamic principles, and should they work with other scientists to develop modern science further?

A POSSIBLE MEETING POINT

Science is not alien to Muslim society, as can be seen from the large numbers of brilliant Muslim scientists that it produced in the past. Given this, there is no reason why its correct use by Muslims cannot help them be better Muslims and more comfortable citizens of the world. It is important to stress that modern science, as it exists today, is not the product of the West alone but contains the contributions of historical Muslim scientists, many of whom still command respect in the global scientific community. According to Hoodbhoy:

> What has happened today is that the West has taken over the leadership of science and reduced it to its present anti-people state in which it dictates the lives of individuals ... and enters even into human relationships.[59]

That science has now "gone bad" would be a bad reason for Muslims to abandon their predecessors' contributions and start over. They have the Divine guidance and can use it to set science on the correct path once again. But this should not be a license for Muslims to become idle consumers of Western technology, checking it only for what is allowed (*halal*) and prohibited (*haram*). With the hints and encouragement of the Qur'an, Muslims should exert themselves and make original contributions to scientific research, investing it, as they go along, with Islamic doctrinal direction and moral values. Otherwise, how can their complaints against modern science's hostility to religion continue to be valid when they have allowed others to lead, dominate, and control it?

Science has been neglected at many levels: at the level of ordinary Muslims who should get involved in scientific research, at the level of the religious leadership who should encourage believers to study science, and at the level of the political leadership who should follow the example of their predecessors, such as Caliph Mu'taqid and other leaders who supported such research.

Professor Mohammed Abdus Salam, winner of the 1979 Nobel Prize, has expressed his concern about such neglect:

> I have been asking the Ulama why their sermons should not exhort Muslims to take up the subjects of science and technology, considering that one-eighth of the Holy Book speaks of *taffakur* and *taskhir—science* and technology.[60]

His other arguments imply that Islam can offer guidance and stimulus in matters of accurate scientific observation, but that the results must be demonstrably objective, and that Muslims are just as capable of achieving this as any one else—if not better. He says:

> We [Abdus Salam and the other two scientists with whom he was coawarded the Prize] were "geographically and ideologically remote from each other" when we conceived the same theory of physics for unifying the weak and the electromagnetic forces. If there was any bias towards the unification paradigm in my thinking, it was unconsciously motivated by my background as a Muslim.[61]

Finally, it is important to stress that a particular locality's sociopolitical and economic realities are important for scientific progress. According to Soliman, Islam provides for a social, political, and economic system that would allow scientists to work in tranquillity, under state protection and sponsorship, and produce results such as those produced in the Muslim world before the split between leaders and scientists.[62] This means that some of the conditions necessary for scientific progress are extra-scientific. The leaders of the Muslim world need to establish a system that enables their scientists to work with security and comfort. When Muslims do this, they will not have to complain about the irreligiousness of modern science because they will be at the forefront.

CONCLUSION

I would like to conclude by stressing the following points:

- Muslims believe that all knowledge is the property of God, Who has given all people the duty and ability to seek, obtain, and use part of this knowledge to better their conditions while they are here as God's vicegerents. Scientific knowledge is part of this general body of knowledge, and it awaits discovery by people willing to exert themselves in search of it.

- Earlier Muslim scientists were diligent searchers of knowledge. Today they are honored even by those who would be happy to believe that they never existed. Even those who are not acknowledged form part of the foundation upon which modern science has been built.

- The Qur'an offers Divine guidance but is not a textbook of science. Attempts to use it as such only gratify those who long to prove its "inadequacy." Likewise, it is sacred and cannot be tested for accuracy, as Khalifa attempts with his "theory of 19."

- Belief is the most precious possession of each Muslim and cannot be discarded, even at the zenith of scientific achievement.

- Western scientists have overstepped the limits in their uses of the results of modern scientific research. Disbelief in God, low levels of morality, and humanity's subjection to machines and mechanical processes are grave developments. It is regrettable that they are associated with the otherwise dignified and indispensable activity of scientific research.

The state of science in Muslim countries is unfortunate, especially given their glorious scientific history. One reason for this is that present leaders of Muslim countries do not follow the example of their predecessors in facilitating scientific research.

• Modern science, as we know it today, was built over a long period and contains contributions from scientists of various civilizations. Islamic civilization was a major contributor to this development. When Muslims use the allowed facilities of modern science, or when Muslim countries borrow technology developed by modern science, they are simply getting back a bit of their own by participating in the age-old practice of technology transfer that took al-Muradi's water-clock to Europe.

Remember that Islam accepted and still lives side-by-side with those aspects of culture and achievement that do not contradict its creed. But Muslim scientists still have the challenge of making original contributions like their predecessors. They should not be content with "discovering" embryology and astronomy in the Qur'an long after their discovery by modern scientists. Armed with Qur'anic guidance, Muslim scientists can lead and guide the general process of scientific research. It need not be *Islamic* science in the sense of starting again and going it alone. However, it must be a science that recognizes the value of positive aspects of previous research—but purged of atheism, infused with moral principles, and practiced in God's name in order to serve humanity.

Scientists of all—or of no—religious convictions will continue to form one family of knowledge seekers. However, with genuine Muslim leadership, modern science's vices can be checked so that the world can enjoy its danger-free benefits and so that the Muslim world finally can solve the "problem" of modern science. This will require men and women with courage and the highest commitment to both Islam and science.

ADDITIONAL SOURCES

- *Bulletin of the Islamic Medical Association of South Africa* (BIMA), vol. 6, no. 1 (April 1985): 1-2.
- Bucaille, Maurice. "The Qur'an and Science" (pamphlet). 1989.
- Chandler, Robert F. Jr. *An Adventure in Applied Science.* Manila: International Rice Research Institute, 1982.
- Al-Daffa, Ali A. and John J. Stroyls. *Studies in the Exact Sciences in Medieval Islam.* Chichester, UK: John Wiley & Sons, 1984.
- Hott, Edwin P. *Arab Science.* Nashville: Thomas Nelson Ltd., 1975.
- Kennedy, E. S. *Studies in the Islamic Exact Sciences.* Beirut: American Univ. in Beirut, 1983.
- Khalifa, Rashid, *Miracle of the Qur'an.* St. Louis: Islamic Productions International, 1973.
- _____. (1982a), Qur'an: Visual Presentation of a Miracle, Islamic Productions International, Tucson (Arizona).
- _____. (1982b), Qur'an, Hadith and Islam, Islamic Productions International, Tucson (Arizona).
- Khuda, Manzoori-i. *Muslim Perspective* (March 1985). Masjid Tucson.
- Nasr, Seyyed Hossein. *Traditional Islam in the Modern World.* London: Kegan and Paul Ltd., 1987.
- _____. *An Introduction to Islamic Cosmological Doctrines.* Bath: Thames and Hudson Ltd., 1978.
- _____. *Islamic Science: An Illustrated Study.* London: World of Islam Festival, 1976.
- _____. *The Encounter of Man and Nature: The Spiritual Crisis of Modern Man.* London: Allen and Unwin, 1968 .
- Negus, Yunus. "Science Within Islam," in Khalid, Fazlun and Joanne O'Brien (eds.). *Islam and Ecology.* New York: Cassell Publishers Ltd., 1992.
- Ibn Rushd, Muhammad. *Tahafut al-Tahafut* (The Incoherence of the Incoherence). trans. S. Van den Bergh. vol. 1. London: E. J. W. Gibb Memorial Series, 1969 edn.
- Sardar, Ziyauddin. *The Future of Muslim Civilizations.* London: Mansell, 1987.
- Said, Hakim Mohammed. *Al-Biruni Commemorative Volume.* Karachi: Hamdard Academy, 1979.
- Swartz, Melin L. *Studies in Islam.* London: Oxford Univ. Press, 1981.
- Williams, Trevor I. (ed.). *A Biographical Dictionary of Scientists.* London: Adam & Charles Black Ltd., 1969.

SCIENCE AND RELIGION

M. Fethullah Gülen & Ali Ünal

Whether the Qur'an refers explicitly or implicitly to scientific facts, and the exact relationship between the Qur'an and modern science, are matters of considerable controversy among Muslim intellectuals. Therefore, we will discuss this subject at some length.

SCIENCE AND RELIGION

Science considers any fact established through empirical methods to be scientific. Therefore, assertions not established through observation and experiment are only theories or hypotheses.

As science cannot be sure about the future, it does not make definite predictions. Doubt is the basis of scientific investigation. However Prophet Muhammad, who was taught by the All-Knowing, made many decisive predictions. Most have come true already; the rest are waiting for their time to come true. Many Qur'anic verses point to recently discovered and established scientific facts. As pointed out earlier, the Qur'an mentions many important issues of creation and natural phenomena that even the most intelligent person living 14 centuries ago could not have known. Furthermore, it uses the Prophets' miracles to allude to the farthest reaches of science, which originated in the Knowledge of the All-Knowing One.

THE CIVILIZATION THAT ISLAM CREATED

The conflict of science and religion in the West dates back to the thirteenth century. The essential character of the Catholic Church's version of Christianity caused nature to be condemned as a veil separating humanity from God and cursed the knowledge of nature. As a result, science did not advance during the Middle Ages (known as the Dark Ages in European history).

However, during the same period a magnificent civilization was flourishing in the Muslim East. Obeying the Qur'anic injunctions, Muslims studied the Book of Divine Revelation (the Qur'an) and the Book of Creation (the universe) and founded the most magnificent civilization of human history. Scholars from all over the Old World benefited from the centers of higher learning at Damascus, Bukhara, Baghdad, Cairo, Fez, Qairawan, Zeitona, Cordoba, Sicily, Isfahan, Delhi, and elsewhere throughout the Muslim world. Historians liken the Muslim world of that time to a beehive, for roads were full of students, scientists, and scholars traveling from one center of learning to another. Such world-renowned figures as al-Kindi, al-Khwarizmi, al-Farabi, Ibn Sina, al-Mas'udi, Ibn al-Haytham, al-Biruni, al-Ghazali, Nasir al-Din al-Tusi, al-Zahrawi and many others shone like stars in the firmament of the sciences.

In his multi-volume *Introduction to the History of Science* (1927-48), George Sarton divided his work into 50-year periods, naming each chapter after that period's most eminent scientist. From the middle of the eighth century CE/second century AH to the twelfth century CE/fifth century AH, each of the seven 50-year periods carries the name of a Muslim scientist: "the Time of al-Khwarizmi," "the Time of al-Biruni," and so on. Within these chapters, Sarton lists 100 important Muslim scientists and their principal works.

John Davenport, a leading scientist, observed:

> It must be owned that all the knowledge whether of Physics, Astronomy, Philosophy or Mathematics, which flourished in Europe from the 10th century was originally derived from the Arabian schools, and the Spanish Saracen may be looked upon as the father of European philosophy.[1]

Bertrand Russell, the famous British philosopher, wrote:

> The supremacy of the East was not only military. Science, philosophy, poetry, and the arts, all flourished in the Muhammadan world at a time when Europe was sunk in barbarism. Europeans, with unpardonable insularity, call this period "the Dark Ages": but it was only in Europe that it was dark—indeed only in Christian Europe, for Spain, which was Muhammadan, had a brilliant culture.[2]

Robert Briffault, the renowned historian, acknowledges in his *The Making of Humanity*:

> It is highly probable that but for the Arabs, modern European civilization would have never assumed that character which has enabled it to transcend all previous phases of evolution. For although there is not a single aspect of human growth in which the decisive influence of Islamic culture is not traceable, nowhere is it so clear and momentous as in the genesis of that power which constitutes the paramount distinctive force of the modern world and the supreme course of its victory—natural sciences and the scientific spirit... What we call sciences arose in Europe as a result of a new spirit of inquiry; of new methods of investigation, of the method of experiment, observation, measurement, of the development of Mathematics in a form unknown to the Greeks. That spirit and those methods were introduced into the European world by the Arabs.[3]

L. Stoddard acknowledges that for its first 5 centuries, the realm of Islam was the most civilized and progressive portion of the world. Studded with splendid cities, gracious mosques, and quiet universities, the Muslim East offered a striking contrast to the West, which was sunk in the night of the Dark Ages.[4]

This bright civilization progressed until it suffered terrible disasters coming like huge overlapping waves: the European Crusades (1097-1270) and the Mongol invasion (1216-58). These disasters continued for centuries, until the Muslim government in Baghdad collapsed (1258) and the history of Islam entered a new phase in the thirteenth century with the Ottoman Turks.

Islamic civilization was still vigorous and remained far ahead of the West in economic and military fields until the eighteenth century, despite (from the sixteenth century onward) losing ground to it in the sciences.

In the tenth century, Muslim Cordoba was Europe's most civilized city, the wonder and admiration of the world. Travelers from the north heard with something like fear of the city that contained 70 libraries with hundreds of thousands of volumes and 900 public baths. Whenever the rulers of Leon, Navarre, or Barcelona needed a surgeon, architect, dressmaker, or musician, they contacted Cordoba.[5] Muslim literary prestige was so great in Spain that the Bible and the liturgy had to be translated into Arabic for the indigenous Christian community. The account given by Alvaro, a zealous Christian writer, shows vividly how even non-Muslim Spaniards were attracted to Arab/Muslim literature:

> My fellow Christians delight in the poems and romances of the Arabs. They study the works of Muhammadan theologians and philosophers, not in order to refute them, but to acquire a correct and elegant Arabic style. Where today can a layman be found who reads the Latin commentaries on holy Scriptures? Who is there that studies the Gospels, the Prophets, the Apostles? Alas, the young Christians who are the most conspicuous for their talents have no knowledge of any literature or language save the Arabic; they read and study with avidity Arabian books; they amass whole libraries of them at a vast cost, and they everywhere sing the praises of the Arabian world.[6]

If the purpose of education and civilization is to raise people's pride, dignity, and honor so that they can improve their state and consequently the state of society, Islamic civilization has proven its value. Many writers have discussed Islam's ability to transform the societies with which it comes into contact. For example, in his speech delivered at the Church Congress of England about Islam's effects and influence upon people, Isaac Taylor said:

> When Muhammadanism is embraced, paganism, fetishism, infanticide and witchcraft disappear. Filth is replaced by cleanliness

and the new convert acquires personal dignity and self-respect. Immodest dances and promiscuous intercourse of the sexes cease; female chastity is rewarded as a virtue; industry replaces idleness; licence gives place to law; order and sobriety prevail; blood feuds, cruelty to animals and slaves are eradicated. Islam swept away corruption and superstitions. Islam was a revolt against empty polemics. It gave hope to the slave, brotherhood to mankind, and recognition to the fundamental facts of human nature. The virtues which Islam inculcates are temperance, cleanliness, chastity, justice, fortitude, courage, benevolence, hospitality, veracity and resignation ... Islam preaches a practical brotherhood, the social equality of all Muslims. Slavery is not part of the creed of Islam. Polygamy is a more difficult question. Moses did not prohibit it. It was practised by David and it is not directly forbidden in the New Testament. Muhammad limited the unbounded licence of polygamy. It is the exception rather than the rule ... In resignation to God's Will, temperance, chastity, veracity and in brotherhood of believers they (the Muslims) set us a pattern which we should do well to follow. Islam has abolished drunkenness, gambling and prostitution, the three curses of the Christian lands. Islam has done more for civilization than Christianity. The conquest of one-third of the earth to his (Muhammad's) creed was a miracle.[7]

SCIENCE AND THE MODERN SCIENTIFIC APPROACH

We have given a lengthy introduction to this subject to clarify one aspect: the conflicting attitudes in the Muslim world about the relationship of Islam and science.

For many years, swayed by Western dominion over their lands, a dominion attributed to superior science and technology, some Muslim intellectuals accused Islam itself as [being] the cause of the backwardness of Muslim peoples. Having forgotten the 11 centuries or more of Islamic supremacy, they thought and wrote as if the history of Islam had only begun in the eighteenth century. Further, they made the deplorable mistake of identifying the relationship between science and religion in general in the specific terms of the relationship between science and

Christianity. They did not bother to make even a superficial study of Islam and its long history.

In contrast to this, other contemporary Muslim intellectuals follow some of their Western counterparts in condemning science and technology outright and adopt an almost purely idealistic attitude. They do this after seeing the disasters—atomic bombs, mass murders, environmental pollution, loss of all moral and spiritual values, the "delirium" from which modern people suffer, and so on—that science and technology have brought to humanity, the shortcomings and mistakes of the purely scientific approach has made in seeking the truth, and the failure of science and technology to bring humanity happiness. However, Islam is the middle way. It does not reject, condemn, or "deify" the modern scientific approach.

Science has been the most revered fetish or idol of modern people for nearly 200 years. Scientists once believed that they could explain every phenomenon through science and the law of causality. However, modern physics destroyed the theoretical foundations of mechanical physics and revealed that the universe is not a clockwork of certain parts working according to strict, unchanging laws of causality and absolute determinism. Rather, despite its dazzling harmony and magnificent order, it is so complex and indeterminate that unveiling one mystery causes many more appear. Thus the more we learn about the universe, the greater our ignorance of it becomes.

Experts in atomic physics say that no one can be sure that the universe will be in the same state a moment later as it is in now. Although the universe works according to certain laws, these laws are not absolute and, more interestingly, have no real or material existence. Rather, their existence is nominal, for we deduce them by observing natural events and phenomena.

Also, it is highly questionable to what extent they have a part in [the] creation and working of things. For example, scientists say that a seed, soil, air and water bring a tree into existence, although they are causes for this result. A tree's existence requires exact calculations and ratios and the pre-established relations of the seed, soil, air and water. Science should explain how this process begins and how the seeds have become diversified. But all it does is explain how things take place, thinking it has explained the origin of existence by attributing it to nature, self-origination, necessity, or chance.

> Nature is a print or a model composed of unseen laws, but not a printer and composer. It is a design, not the designer; a recipient, not the agent; an order, not the one who puts in order. It is a collection of laws established by Divine Will, laws [that our minds can grasp but] that in themselves have no power or material reality.[8]

Attribution of existence to self-origination, necessity, or chance is delusion, for we can see that existence displays absolute knowledge, absolute wisdom, absolute will, and absolute power. Self-origination, necessity, and chance are only concepts without any material reality, and therefore cannot possess any knowledge, wisdom, will, or power.

The modern scientific approach is far from finding out and explaining the truth behind existence. Truth is unchanging and beyond the visible world. Its relationship with the visible, changing world is like that of the spirit and the body, of the Divine laws of nature and natural things and events. For example, the force of growth (a universal Divine law) is innate in all living things. It is unchanging, and yet a tree or a person is always changing. Likewise, regardless of how our clothing, houses, or means of transport change over time, we remain unchanged in terms of our essential purposes and needs as well as their impact upon our lives and environments. All people share certain general conditions of life and value: birth, maturity, marriage, children, and death. We all possess some degree of will and common desires and, moreover, share certain values: honesty, kindness, justice, courage, and so on.

Despite these facts, the modern scientific approach searches for truth in changing nature and bases itself upon our senses' impressions. But these impressions are deceptive and relative, for they change from person to person. Also, not all people have the same ability to reason. Thus it is impossible to arrive at one certain conclusion by applying deductive, inductive, or analytical reasoning to sense-based data. This is why the modern scientific approach tries to reach facts through experimentation. However, without pre-established axioms or premises, experiments cannot establish a fact.

Since the time of Hume,[9] it has been generally accepted that just because an event has happened twice or a million times in two or a million different places, it must happen again. For this reason, since the collapse of classical physics Western epistemologists have spoken not of seeking the truth itself, but of seeking approximations of it. Popper[10] says that we consider Newton's and Einstein's theories as science... both of them cannot be true at the same time; rather, both may be false.

Science cannot find the truth of existence's essence through empirical methods. Therefore, as Guénon puts it, science or scientists must either acknowledge that science's findings are no more than suppositions about truth and thus not recognize any certainty higher than sense perception, or blindly believe as true whatever is taught in the name of science.[11] Doubting the findings of science, modern scientists try to find a way out via agnosticism or pragmatism, thus confessing the inability of science to find truth.

Science should recognize its limits and concede that truth is unchanging and lies in the realm above the visible world. Doing so would allow it to find its real value. The relative cannot exist without the absolute. Change is possible only if the unchanging exists, and multiplicity is possible only if unity exists. Knowledge acquires permanence and stability only when it reaches the point of immutability. What is unchangeable and permanent is above the human realm. Truth is not something produced by the human mind, for it exists independently of us. Our task is to seek it.

CONFLICT BETWEEN RELIGION AND SCIENCE?

Seeing religion and science or scientific studies as two conflicting disciplines is a product of the Western attitude toward religion and science. To understand this conflict, first we will discuss how science developed in the West.

While doing this, however, we should remember that the main reason for this scientific progress was the influence of Islamic civilization. Since this fact has been mentioned above, we will concentrate upon three other factors: changes in Western thinking, Protestantism, and geographical discoveries and colonialism.

CHRISTIANITY AND THE CHANGING WESTERN WAY OF THINKING: When Christianity became the Roman Empire's state religion,[12] after years of struggle and the lives of thousands of martyrs, it found itself in a climate of prevalent Epicurean and naturalistic attitudes and sanctified human knowledge.

Jesus' teaching, subsequently known as Christianity, defeated the Roman Empire at the expense of certain doctrinal compromise. It restricted itself to love and condemned nature as a veil separating humanity from God. It embarked on the path of becoming a completely mystical religion. However, Islam and all God-revealed religions see Earth or nature as a realm in which God's Most Beautiful Names are manifested, upon which minds should reflect in order to reach God Almighty, and in which Paradise is reflected.

The Church, proclaiming itself the body of Christ and thereby enjoying his authority, shaped Christianity as explained above and later sought worldly power. While Europe was ruled by the Church, a magnificent civilization flourished in the Muslim East. As a result of Europe's contact with this civilization through the Crusades and Andalusia (Muslim Spain), Europe learned about Antiquity. Greek philosophy (especially Aristotelianism), Epicurism, and hedonism, as well as Roman naturalism, found their way into European thought. When this awakening to Antiquity via translations from Arabic and Muslim centers of learning in Andalusia and Sicily was united with Europe's envy of the Muslim East's prosperity, the ground was prepared for the Renaissance.

European ways of thinking changed greatly. The Church's centuries-old "iron wall" between European attitudes and Islam, as well as its view that such new ways of thinking threatened its worldly power, engendered a hostile reaction to religion. The emerging intelligentsia could not find answers in the Bible to the questions posed by new developments in science and changing world-view. Besides, they thought some of the passages to be contradictory with these developments.

For example, the Old Testament mentions 7 days like the days of the world when describing creation: *And there was evening, and there was morning—the first day* (Genesis 1:5). But the conception of a day as consisting of a morning and an evening is a human concept. The Qur'an also mentions days and that God created the universe in 6 days, but without specifying any mornings or evenings. Moreover, it presents *day* as a relative period of unknown duration:

> The angels and spirit ascend to Him in a day whereof the span is 50,000 years. (70:4)

> They will bid you hasten on the Doom, and God fails not His promise, but a day with God is 1,000 years of what you reckon. (22:47)

> He directs the affair from the heaven unto Earth; then it ascends unto Him in a Day, whereof the measure is 1,000 years of what you reckon. (32:5)

There are many other factors which caused science to develop in opposition to religion. However, such great scientists as Galileo and Bacon were not irreligious; all they wanted was a new interpretation of the Bible. Certain scientists and theologians tried to do this. For example, Bacon favored experimental methods in scientific investigations and defended the idea that one could attain knowledge of heavenly things through spiritual experience. Thomas Aquinas,[13] whom some introduce as the Christian counterpart of Imam Ghazali, tried to reconcile Christianity with Aristotelianism. Another theologian, Nicolas de Cusa,[14] opposed Ptolemaic astronomy but stressed the profound meaning of the limitless universe, whose center is everywhere and whose peripheries are nowhere. Nevertheless, the efforts of such theologians and scientists to reconcile Christianity with science could not prevent science from finally breaking with religion. The Church's intense opposition to scientific developments and Europe's gradual awakening to materialism were just too strong for Christianity.

As Professor Tawney says, medieval people usually sought eternal happiness through economic activities and enterprises, and feared economic motives that appeared in the form of strong desires. A man had the right to gain enough money to lead a life according to his social status, but to try to gain more meant greed and was considered a grave sin. Wealth and property had to be obtained legally through lawful ways and circulate among as many people as possible.[15]

But the Renaissance changed social or even moral standards. We also can say that such changes gave birth to the Renaissance. A superficial glance at that period's art reveals this fundamental change from the moral and spiritual to the material. For example, sculpture, which Sorokin[16] considers to be produced by a desire to escape death and the mental "disease" of representing mortals in the shape of young, immortal deities, used the female body to model passionate desires and pleasures, deceit, sexuality and physical beauty. In Renaissance art, the Virgin Mary was no longer an image of modesty and chastity inspiring respect and compassion, but gradually was transformed into a woman with physical charms. Michelangelo's David is a powerful, muscular, and naked youth, a representation of bodily perfection.

The Renaissance man desired to be like Odysseus[17]: well-built, comely, intelligent, powerful, and skilled in oratory. He was convinced that this was possible through knowledge. Nevertheless, the "God" of the Bible was jealous and forbade humanity to eat of the fruit of knowledge:

> The Lord God took the man and put him in the Garden of Eden to work it and take care of it. And the Lord God commanded the man: "You are free to eat from any tree in the garden; but you must not eat from the tree of the knowledge of good and evil, for when you eat of it you will surely die." (Genesis 2:15-17)

> And the Lord God said: "[By eating of the tree of the knowledge of good and evil], the man has now become like one of us, knowing good and evil. He must not be allowed to reach out his hand and take also from the tree of life and eat, and live for ever." So the Lord God banished him from the Garden of Eden to work the ground from which he had been taken. (Genesis 3:22-23)

These Biblical verses would be sources of antipathy to a typical Renaissance man and remind him of the Greek deities who kept the sacred fire from humanity. Thus Prometheus, who rebelled against the gods and stole their sacred fire, fired their imaginations. This change of attitude toward religion and life is a primary point in understanding the conflict between science and religion in the West.

PROTESTANTISM: According to Weber, science and technology in the West did not develop independently, for one of its driving forces was Protestantism. This Christian sect, originally a rebellion against the Catholic Church's authority, did not radically depart from Christian dogma.

Weber wrote that Protestantism is fatalistic toward history and human destiny. Everybody is born with Original Sin, and no one can be saved from eternal condemnation by his or her own deeds. Both Luther and Calvin[18] opined that God has destined only certain chosen people to be saved from eternal punishment.

Such a status is indicated by that person's tireless work and continuous activity to overcome feelings of weakness and helplessness. In other words, one's wealth and success indicate how much one is loved by God. Weber asserts that the middle class' grudge against the rich and the aristocracy roused them to further earning and wealth accumulation. Earning incited consumption, consumption produced endless need, and need stimulated further work. In Weber's words, this never-ending spiral played an important role in scientific and technological progress. However, it is also behind the egotism, individualism, and self-centeredness of modern people.

GEOGRAPHIC DISCOVERIES AND COLONIALISM: Royal despotism and feudalism, when united with Church authority, suffocated people. Seemingly unable to meet their increasing needs and having easy access to oceans, Europeans began to venture overseas. Needs urge people to investigate and learn new things, and natural ways of transportation (rivers and seas) enable people in small lands to make frequent contact with surrounding and overseas lands.

The Europeans of the Renaissance embraced this chance to increase their knowledge and reach remote lands. They pursued gold, and became greedy and cruel wherever they found it. These were the people who opened the way to a ruthless colonialism. The slave trade and the almost total extermination of the indigenous peoples of America, Australia, and elsewhere became the trademark of rising capitalism and colonialism. Only after transporting the treasures of the newly invaded and conquered lands to Europe could the Industrial Revolution occur. All historians agree that James Watt invented the steamship after Bengal's (India) coal was taken to England after the Battle of Plassey (1757). The invention of the steamship (1809) marked the start of the Industrial Revolution. Today, the United States, whose population forms only 6% of the world's population, consumes 40% of the world's paper pulp, 36% of its coal, 25% of its steel, and 20% of its cotton.

The developed countries together form only 16% of the world's population, yet consume 80% of its resources.

In sum, remember that a ruthless colonialism and geographic discoveries are two of the main factors behind Europe's scientific and technological advances.

DOES THE QUR'AN CONTAIN EVERYTHING?

> With Him are the keys of the Unseen. None but He knows them. And He knows what is in the land and the sea. Not a leaf falls but with His Knowledge, not a grain amid the darkness of the earth, nothing of wet or dry but (it is noted) in a Manifest Book. (6:59)

Ibn Mas'ud says that the Qur'an provides information on everything, but that we may not be able to see everything in it. Ibn 'Abbas, the "Interpreter of the Qur'an" and "Scholar of the Umma," asserts that if he loses his camel's rein, he can find it by means of the Qur'an. Jalal al-Din al-Suyuti, a major scholar who lived in Egypt in the 15th century CE, explains that all sciences or branches of knowledge can be found in the Qur'an.

How can a medium-sized book, which also contains a great deal of repetition, contain everything we need to know about life, science, conduct, creation, past and future, and so on?

Before explaining this important matter, we should point out that to benefit from the Qur'an, which transcends time and location and is not bound by its audience's intellectual level, we have to prepare ourselves to do so. We should have firm belief in it and do our best to implement its principles in our daily life. We must refrain from sin as much as possible. As the Qur'an declares we only get what we strive for (53:39), we should, like a deep-sea explorer, dive into its "ocean" and, without becoming tired or bored, continue studying it until we die.

Moreover, we need a good command of Arabic and sufficient knowledge of all branches of the natural and religious sciences. A good interpretation necessitates cooperation among scientists from all natural and social sciences, and religious scholars who are experts in Qur'anic commentary, Hadith (Traditions), *fiqh* (Islamic jurisprudence), theology, and spiritual sciences. While reciting and studying the Qur'an, we should regard it as if we were its first addressees, consciously aware that each verse addresses us directly. If we consider, for example, its historical accounts of the Prophets and their peoples as unrelated to us, we will derive no benefit.

According to its nature and significance, worth and place in existence, everything has its own place in the Qur'an. The Qur'an contains everything, but not to the same degree. It pursues four purposes: to prove the Existence and Unity of God, Prophethood, bodily resurrection, and worship of God and justice.

To realize its purposes, the Qur'an draws our attention to God's acts in the universe, His matchless art displayed through creation, the manifestations of His Names and Attributes, and the perfect order and harmony seen in existence. It mentions certain historical events and establishes the rules of personal and social good conduct and morality, as well as the principles of a happy, harmonious social life. In addition, it explains how to worship and please our Creator, gives us some information about the next life, and tells us how to gain eternal happiness and be saved from eternal punishment.

Everything is contained in the Qur'an, but at different levels. Therefore, not everything is readily apparent. The Qur'an's main duty is to teach about God's Perfection, Essential Qualities, and acts, as well as our duties, status, and how to serve Him. Thus it contains them as seeds or nuclei, summaries, principles, or signs that are explicit or implicit, allusive or vague, or suggestive. Each occasion has its own form and is presented in the best way for making each Qur'anic purpose known according to the existing requirements and context.

For example: Human progress in science and industry has brought about such scientific and technological wonders as airplanes, electricity, motorized transport, and radio and telecommunication, all of which have become basic and essential for our modern, materialistic civilization. The Qur'an has not ignored them and points to them in two ways:

- The first is, as will be explained below, by way of the Prophets' miracles.
- The second concerns certain historical events. In other words, the wonders of human civilization only merit a passing reference, an implicit reference, or an allusion in the Qur'an.

For example, if an aircraft told the Qur'an: "Give me the right to speak and a place in your verses," the aircrafts of the sphere of Divine Lordship (the planets, Earth, the moon) would reply on the Qur'an's behalf: "You may take a place here in proportion to your size." If a submarine asked for a place, the submarines belonging to that sphere, the heavenly bodies "swimming" in the atmosphere's vast "ocean" would say: "Compared to us, you are invisible." If shining, star-like electric lights demanded the right to be included, the electric lights of that sphere (lightning, shooting stars, and stars adorning the sky's face) would reply: "Your right to be mentioned and spoken about is proportional to your light."

If the wonders of human civilization demanded a place based on the fineness of their art, a single fly would reply: "O be quiet! Even my wing has more right than you. If all of humanity's fine arts and delicate instruments were banded together, the delicate members of my tiny body would still be more wonderful and exquisite. The verse: *Those upon whom you call, apart from God, shall never create (even) a fly, though they banded together to do it* (22:73), will silence you."

The Qur'an's viewpoint of life and the world is completely different from the modern one. It sees the world as a guest-house, and people as temporary guests preparing themselves for eternal life by undertaking their most urgent and important duties. As that which is designed and used mostly for worldly purposes only has a tiny share in servanthood to and worship of God, which is founded upon love of truth and otherworldliness, it therefore has a place in the Qur'an according to its merit.

The Qur'an does not explicitly mention everything necessary for our happiness in this world and the next for another reason: Religion is a divine test to distinguish elevated and base spirits from each other. Just as raw materials are refined to separate diamonds from coal and gold from soil, religion tests conscious beings to separate precious "ore" in the "mine" of human potential from dross.

Since the Qur'an was sent to perfect us, it only alludes to those future events pertaining to the world, which everyone will see at the appropriate time, and only opens the door to reason to the degree necessary to prove its argument. If everything was explicit, the test would be meaningless, for the truth of the Divine obligations would be readily apparent. Given that we would then be unable to deny or ignore them, the competition behind our testing and trials would be unnecessary, for we would have to confirm their truth. "Coal" spirits would remain with and appear to be no different from "diamond" spirits.

As the great majority of people are always "average," the Qur'an uses a style and language that everyone can understand. An ordinary person and a great scientist can benefit from the Qur'an, regardless of his or her specialization. A most suitable way to do this is through symbols, metaphors and allegories, comparisons and parables. Those well-versed in knowledge (3:7) know how to approach and benefit from the Qur'an, and conclude that it is the Word of God.

Earlier civilizations would neither have benefited from nor understood Qur'anic accounts of modern scientific and technological discoveries, so why mention them? Also, scientific "truths" change constantly and therefore are not eternal.

God Almighty gave us intelligence, and the Qur'an urges us to use it to study ourselves, nature, and surrounding events. If it mentioned modern scientific and technological discoveries or everything pertaining to life, nature, history, and humanity, creating us in our present form would have been pointless. God created us as the best pattern of creation, and gave us many intellectual faculties. But if everything were clear, we would not need these, for we would already know everything.

Finally, if the Qur'an contained explicit references to everything we want to know, it would be so large that its complete recitation would be impossible. We would be unable to benefit from its spiritual enlightenment, and would become really bored while reciting it. Such results contradict the reasons for the Qur'an's revelation and its purposes.

THE CONCEPT OF SCIENCE AND TECHNOLOGY

Despite the disasters caused by science and technology, their mistaken approach to the truth, and their failure to bring human happiness, we cannot condemn them outright and become pure idealists. Science and technology do not bear the full responsibility for humanity being devalued, human feelings being diminished, and certain human virtues along with health and the ability to think, being seriously weakened. Rather, the fault lies with scientists who avoid their responsibilities, who cause science to develop in a materialistic and almost purely scientific atmosphere, and then let it be exploited by an irresponsible minority. Many worrying conditions probably would not exist if scientists had remained aware of their social responsibility, and if the Church had not forced it to develop in opposition to religion.

Flowing to the future like a rapid flood full of energy and vitality, and sometimes resembling a dazzling garden, the natural world is like a book for us to study, an exhibition to behold, and a trust from which we can benefit. We are responsible for studying the meaning and content of this trust so that we and future generations may benefit from it. If we wish, we can call this relationship "science."

Science also can be described as comprehending what things and events tell us, what the Divine laws reveal to us, and striving to understand the Creator's purpose. Created to rule creation, we need to observe and read, to discern and learn about our surroundings so that we can find the best way to exert our influence and control. When we reach this level, by the decree of the Exalted Creator, everything will submit to us and we will submit to God.

There is no reason to fear science. The danger does not lie with science and the founding of the new world it will usher in, but rather with ignorance and irresponsible scientists and others who exploit it for their own selfish interests.

If true science directs human intelligence toward eternity without expecting any material gain, undertakes a tireless and detailed study of existence to discover absolute truth, and follows the methods required to reach this aim, what can we say about modern science other than it cannot fulfill our expectations? Although usually presented as a conflict between Christianity and science, the conflicts during the Renaissance were mainly between scientists (not science per se) and the Church. Copernicus, Galileo, and Bacon[19] were not anti-religious; in fact, we could say that their religious commitment drove them toward scientific truth.

Before Christianity it was Islam, the religious thought springing from eternality, and the resulting love and zeal accompanied by feelings of poverty and impotence before the Eternal, All-Powerful and All-Wealthy Creator of the cosmos, that enabled the Muslim world's great five-century scientific advance until the close of the twelfth century CE. Its driving concept of science as based on Divine Revelation was represented almost perfectly by illustrious figures who, imbued with eternality, tirelessly studied existence to attain eternity. Their commitment to Divine Revelation caused It to diffuse a light that engendered a new concept of science in human souls.

If Islamic civilization had not been so badly damaged by the horrific Mongolian (1216-58) and numerous destructive Crusader

(1097-1270) invasions, the world today certainly would be very different. If the Islamic concept of science as being approved and appropriated by the community, as if it were part of the Divine Message and pursued as an act of worship, had continued to flourish, our world would be more enlightened, its intellectual life richer, its technology more wholesome, and its sciences more promising. All Islamic science sought, based on eternality, was to benefit humanity by helping us to aspire for the other world and to handle things responsibly for the sake and pleasure of God Almighty.

Only the love of truth, defined as approaching existence not for material advantage or worldly gain but to observe and recognize it as it really is, gives true direction to scientific studies. Those with such love will achieve their goal; those who do not have such love, who are led by worldly passion, material aspiration, ideological prejudice and fanaticism, either will fail or turn science into a deadly weapon to be used against what is best for humanity.

Intellectuals, educational institutions, and the mass media must strive to deliver modern science from the current lethal atmosphere of materialism and ideological fanaticism. To redirect scientists toward human values, scientists' minds must be freed of ideological superstition and fanaticism and their souls purified of desire for worldly gain and advantage. This will enable them to secure true freedom of thought and engage in good science. Their centuries-long battle against the clergy and corrupt concepts formed in the name of religion, and their subsequent denunciation of religious people as backward, narrow-minded, and fanatic, should serve as a warning to scientists not to fall into the same trap.

Intellectual and scientific despotism arise from a group's own self-interest and power-seeking, ideology and fanaticism. Such groups can be found among both scientists and clerics. Despotism is despotism, whether it arises from restricting reason to corrupt and distorted religious conceptions and clerical domination or its scientific counterpart. Islam continually urges humanity to study nature (the exhibition of Divine works), reflect on creation and what has been created, and approach it responsibly in order to benefit humanity.

When studied without prejudice and preconception, the Qur'an shows that it promotes the love of science and humanity, justice and order. The Qur'an is full of verses urging us to study nature. It also urges us to reflect upon creation and the created, to approach it responsibly, and to use it to everybody's benefit. According to Islam, the whole point of seeking knowledge is to discover the meaning of existence so that we can reach the Creator and benefit humanity and all of creation. And then, we are to combine that knowledge with belief, love, and altruism. Humanity has seen such an ideal in practice: The exemplary life of Prophet Muhammad and the conduct of many of its representatives who perfected their thoughts and deeds.

So what is there to fear from science? Planned acts based on knowledge sometimes cause bad results, but certainly ignorance and disorganization always cause bad results. Instead of opposing the products of science and technology, we must use them to bring happiness to humanity. Herein lies the essence of our greatest problem, for we cannot take measures against the Space Age or erase atomic or hydrogen bomb-making knowledge.

Although science might be a deadly weapon in the hands of an irresponsible minority, we should not hesitate to adopt both science and its products and then use them to establish a civilization in which we can secure our happiness in this world and the next. It is pointless to curse machines and factories, because machines will continue to run and factories to operate. Science and its products will begin to benefit us only when people of truth and belief begin to direct our affairs.

We have never suffered harm from a weapon in the hands of angels. Whatever we have suffered has come from those who still believe that only might is right. This situation will continue until we build a world on a foundation of faith and science.

TWO DIFFERENT FIELDS FOR SCIENCE AND RELIGION?

Christianity did not develop as a comprehensive religion encompassing all fields of life, but as a set of spiritual and moral values with a direct bearing on life's worldly aspects. This has had serious consequences for subsequent Western history. For example, Christianity condemned war but refused to recognize its reality in human history and therefore laid down no rules of conduct for it. Since such an attitude has never ended any war, the lack of religion-based rules for war has resulted in great brutality and ruthless massacres by various Western nations throughout the world.

Similarly, Christianity condemns the world and nature as a veil separating humanity from God, a view that has encouraged modern science to regard religious authority as irrelevant. Also, the dualism apparent in separating this world and the Hereafter, religion and science, spirituality and physicality, led Western thinkers and philosophers who tried to find a space for religion beside science to assign different fields to religion and science, reason and Revelation, this world and the Hereafter.

CARTESIAN DUALISM

Descartes[20] is the person most associated with this Western dualism, for his ideas contributed to the almost complete separation of intellectual and scientific activities from religion and, in later centuries, to the Enlightenment, the mechanistic view of life, positivism, and materialism. Cartesianism provided a shelter for those who separated their search for religion in life from their search for science. It also gave rise to many misconceptions about the relationship among life, religion, and science. Those intellectuals or philosophers who did not want to forsake either religion or scientific reasoning appealed to Cartesian dualism to justify their position.

This manner of defending religion against scientific materialism still prevails among certain Muslim intellectuals. According to them, there is a World of Qualities separate from a World of

Quantities. Science has the authority in the World of Quantities and uses observation, measurement, and experimentation. But in the World of Qualities, where observation, experimentation, and measurement do not apply, religion has the right to speak. Therefore being religious cannot contradict being scientific, for religion and science have nothing to do with each other.

Although intended to defend religion against science, Cartesian dualism makes science superior to religion. By restricting religion to a set of blindly held beliefs, it relegates it to a secondary role in practical life and thought. These beliefs cannot be subjected to research, verification, and reasoning, and thus are practically irrelevant to the world and worldly life. This attitude represents religion as being only a matter of belief or non-belief, which is totally incorrect, and "proves" that there is little difference between accepting a "true" religion and belief in any other religion or even in myths and superstitions. This dualism lies behind modern trends that consider religion, whether God-revealed or human-made, as a set of dogmas inaccessible to reason and cut off from science and the perceptible world.

But religion, especially Islam, demands rational and spiritual conviction based on thinking, reasoning, searching, and verification as opposed to blind belief. Although one can enter religion through the gate of imitation, it is never advisable to remain content with a belief based on imitation. The Qur'anic verses related to legal issues do not exceed 300, while more than 700 verses urge people to study natural phenomena and to think, reason, search, observe, take lessons, reflect, and verify. The verses concluding with: *Will you not use your reason?; Will you not think?; Will you not reflect?; Will you not take lessons?; Take lessons, O people of insight,* and the Qur'anic condemnation of non-believers as people without intellect and therefore unable to think and reflect, without eyes with which to see or ears with which to hear, are serious warnings for those who see religion as blind belief and who cannot discern the essential and unbreakable connection among religion and life, nature, reason, and science.

Modern science studies the natural world. By restricting it to the material, observable realm of existence, Cartesian dualism does not allow it to admit the possibility of other realms of existence and fields of study. This may be regarded as a way of keeping scientific inquiry factual and objective. However, this attitude frequently leads to the view that such non-material studies and their conclusions are unscientific and therefore require only belief instead of research or verification.

It also carries many into agnosticism, to either deny or at least not affirm the more profound and broader dimensions of existence beyond the material. If modern science were truly objective, it either would accept the possibility of many other truths and realms whose existence cannot be discovered by its present methods or change its tactics and techniques and equip itself with the methods necessary to discover those realms. Science will never comprehend the full reality of existence as long as it keeps its rigidly empirical approach and methods. It is unfortunate for science that it reduces humanity and the universe to their physical existence and tries to explain all of our intellectual and spiritual activities in physical terms.

Modern science deals with nature as a structured but aimless or meaningless concurrence of material things. This is not much different from Christianity's condemnation of nature as a veil separating humanity from God. Islam, on the other hand, introduces natural phenomena, as opposed to the supra-natural ones whose existence and reality science either rejects or regards as unknowable by scientific methods, as evidence of its truth or reality. It calls people to study and reflect on them and thereby collect the nectar of belief.

Islam views nature as the realm in which God's Beautiful Names are manifested as a set of "ladders of light" by which to reach God. Having originated from God's Attributes of Will and

Power, nature is the created counterpart of the Qur'an, which originated in the Divine Attribute of Speech. So nature is a book like the Qur'an, a city or palace whose meaning is explained by a sacred pamphlet (the Qur'an). In addition, this sacred pamphlet tells humanity how to dwell in and benefit from nature.

Humanity is the third counterpart of these two books, equipped with consciousness and will. This is why such Muslim scientists as Ibn Sina (Avicenna), Zahrawi, Ibrahim Haqqi, Nasir al-Din al-Tusi, and Ak Shamsaddin were practising Sufis and well-versed in religious sciences.

NATURE DISPLAYS DIVINE UNITY

Nature, the result of the Divine Beautiful Names' manifestations and a collection of mirrors reflecting the Divine Names and Attributes, has a certain sanctity. In fact, its order and constancy are two significant proofs of Divine Unity as well as the roots of all sciences. The universe's perfect order is due to its being the work of a Single Creator, for only this fact can explain the inter-relatedness, cooperation, and solidarity among all of its parts and creatures. For example, an apple can come into existence only if the soil, air, water, and sun, as well as the apple seed's and tree's properties (e.g., germination, growth, photosynthesis, and bearing fruit) fulfill their specific roles. This means that an apple can exist only if the entire universe cooperates.

Scientists classify the order and constancy of whatever takes place in the universe as natural laws, even though the elements or properties of this order and constancy, upon which science is based, have only nominal existence. What science calls laws may well be the works or activities of God through the agency of angels.[21]

Due to its refusal to include religion in its procedures, science attributes the miraculous and purposeful creation and existence, as well as the order, harmony, and constancy prevailing therein, to two things: blind, unconscious, ignorant, and inanimate laws having only nominal existence, or else to nature, which is a passive recipient and not an active agent, an object and not a subject, and devoid of consciousness, knowledge, and will. But such order, harmony, and constancy obviously require the existence of an absolute, eternal knowledge, power, and will.

In addition, science attempts to explain existence and life through chance and necessity. The reason for such ignorance is that science regards religion as a set of dogmas requiring blind belief and therefore as unscientific or irreconcilable with itself. This unforgivable attitude and denial of creation's supra-natural dimension or its agnosticism are the result of separating science and religion.

When separated from religion, science loses its real identity and aim. According to the Qur'an, these are to study existence in the light of Divine guidance in order to understand it, to use the universe as a collection of ladders to reach the "heaven" of belief, and to improve the world and thereby help each person fulfill his or her function of Divine vicegerency on Earth by living in accordance with that belief.

As we read in 2:30-31, when God told the angels He would appoint a vicegerent on Earth, they inferred that corruption, sedition, and bloodshed would result. Why? Because vicegerency requires will, knowledge, and power. Thus they replied: *"We glorify You with Your praise and proclaim Your Holiness." The Almighty answered them: "I know what you know not."* He taught Adam the "names"—the names and reality of things, and thus the keys of knowledge and how to master things.

As He made us superior to angels through this knowledge, He regarded "scientific" studies to understand creation and fulfill our role of vicegerent as equal to the angels' glorification and praise. This means that scientific studies undertaken to understand creation, and thereby recognize the Creator and improve the world by establishing peace and justice, are acts of worship. Given this, Islam clearly gives a sacred meaning and religious dimension to science and scientific studies.

As the first revealed Qur'anic verse begins with *Read!* at a time when written literature and literacy in that area were rare, this command is significant. This order continues: *in the name of the Lord Who creates* (96:1), which means that we should study creation and do so in the Lord's name. The word translated as "Lord" is *Rabb*, One Who brings up, educates, trains, sustains, and raises. This signifies that creation is under God's Lordship and that we should study it thoroughly as regards its coming into existence, growing, and functioning. This is what science does.

The second important connotation is that we should study creation in God's name to please Him and in accordance with His rules. Thus, scientific study should not contradict religious and moral injunctions, harm people, or change the order found in the creation and the universe. When science is used to discover the Divine laws in nature and conducted within the limits of Divine permission, it will not cause environmental pollution, massive death and destruction, or, in short, corruption on Earth. Islam does not prevent scientific studies; rather, it establishes science's moral aims and places moral restrictions upon it. It urges scientists to benefit humanity as well as other creatures and, by ordering them to work in God's name, raises what they do to acts of worship.

Separating science from religion has brought wealth and material well-being to a very small minority. But as the last two centuries have shown, there are some consequences, such as global insecurity, unhappiness, and unease due to the resulting scientific materialism, brutal oppression and colonialism, wide rifts between rich and poor people; unending global or regional wars during which millions die or are left homeless, orphaned, or widowed; merciless class rivalry; and dangerous levels of environmental pollution. Separating science and religion has resulted in numerous disasters.

Another evidence of the inseparability of science and religion, even if denied by secular science, is that Prophets were forerunners of scientific discoveries and material progress. For example, some Qur'anic interpreters infer from: *When Our command came and the boiler started boiling over...* (11:40), that Noah's Ark, constructed through God's guidance, was a steamship. Sailors regard Noah as their first teacher or patron. Similarly, Joseph was the first person to make a clock and thus is considered the first teacher of clock-makers, and Enoch is given the same regard by tailors.

However, secular or materialistic science does not regard Divine Revelation as a source of knowledge or revealed knowledge as scientific. For example, it considers the Flood mentioned in all Divine Scriptures and oral (unwritten) histories of all peoples to be a myth. If this (or any other) event cannot be established through scientific methods, it will not be considered scientific, and those who say that only scientific methods can reach the truth will continue to doubt the Divine Scriptures. This amounts to denying Divine Revelation and all God-revealed religions.

Also, this will cause many historical facts and events to remain hidden, as well as the history of Middle East to be taught inaccurately, for any accurate history of the area must include the life-histories of the Prophets mentioned in the Qur'an. Despite this, secular or materialistic science causes many truths to be taught as falsehoods and many falsehoods to be presented as truths by not admitting that the Divine Revelation possesses scientific reliability. For example, the Assyrians of Iraq are presented as pagans. And yet we read in 37:147: *And We sent him once again to (his people, numbering) 100,000 or more,* that more than 100,000 people believed in Jonah, who, according to the Bible, lived in Nineveh, the Assyrian capital.

Separating science and religion and assigning to each a different realm of competence or relevance has caused religion to be seen as a set of myths and dogmas—blind beliefs—and science to remain in the darkness of materialism. Just as it is absolutely necessary to wed and harmonize the mind and heart or the intellect and spirit, it also is vitally important to harmonize science and religion.

WHAT DOES THE COMMAND *READ!* SIGNIFY?

The first Qur'anic revelation was:

> Read, in and with the Name of your Lord Who created, creat-
> ed human from a clot clinging (to the wall of the womb).
> Read: And your Lord is the All-Munificent, Who has taught by
> the pen, taught man what he knew not. (96:1-3)

This is quite significant, for the unlettered Prophet was told to read at a time when the Book did not yet exist. This means that there is another book or, rather, two books, one being the counterpart to the Book to be revealed: the universe and humanity. Believers should study the universe and humanity without prejudice. In addition, the material and psychological phenomena found in the universe and in humanity also are called signs. The imperative *Read!* is followed by *in and with the name of your Lord Who created*. This signifies three things:

- Reading (studying) the universe has its own principles, such as observation and experiment.

- *Rabb,* translated as "Lord," has many other meanings, among them educator, upbringer, sustainer, giver of a certain pattern, and giver of a particular nature to each entity. Our nature includes free will, whereas every other entity acts according to its assigned primordial nature, which science calls "nature" and the "laws of nature." We are told to discover these laws.

- Every human act, including scientific studies, should be performed in God's name and thus be an act of worship. This is the sole limit that the Qur'an and Islam place upon science. Any act so performed cannot be against God's commandments. For example, if scientific knowledge is pursued as worship, no one could harm humanity or allow an irresponsible minority to use it as a deadly weapon. If done only in His name, and by people aware of His constant supervision and knowing that they will be called to account before a Supreme Tribunal, science could change the world into a Garden of Eden.

Thus, as Nasr emphasizes:

> ... revelation to man is inseparable from the cosmic revelation which is also a book of God. Islam, by refusing to separate man from nature and the study of nature from gnosis or its metaphysical dimension, has preserved an integral view of the universe and sees in the arteries of the cosmic and natural order the flow of Divine grace.[22]

From the bosom of nature, humanity seeks to transcend nature. If people learn how to contemplate nature as a mirror reflecting a higher reality, nature itself can be an aid in this process. This is why Islamic scholars and saints developed an elaborate hierarchy of knowledge (e.g., physical, juridical, social, theological, spiritual, and metaphysical) integrated by the principle of Divine Unity, and why so many Muslim scientists, among them Ibn Sina (Avicenna), Nasir al-Din al-Tusi, Ak Shamsaddin, and Ibrahim Haqqi of Erzurum, were well-versed in religious sciences and either practicing Sufis or intellectually affiliated with Islam's Sufi schools.

Ibn Sina was a physician and Peripatetic philosopher who expounded upon his Oriental philosophy that knowledge could be sought through illumination. Nasir al-Din al-Tusi, the leading mathematician and astronomer of his day, wrote an outstanding treatise on Islam's metaphysical dimension. Eleven centuries ago, Ibn Jarir al-Tabari, one of the most outstanding figures in Islamic jurisprudence, history, and Qur'anic interpretation, wrote how the winds fertilize clouds so that rain falls.

Such examples can be multiplied, but these suffice to show that observing and contemplating nature have always been core aspects of a Muslim's spiritual journey, and that science and other fields of Islamic studies have always been intimately connected. This connection is found in the Qur'an, which, as the Divine Scripture of Islam, corresponds to the macrocosmic revelation— the universe.

DOES THE QUR'AN ALLUDE TO SCIENTIFIC DEVELOPMENTS?

Before answering this question, we should point out one important fact: Considering science as opposed to religion and scientific study as separate from and independent of the Qur'an is just as mistaken as trying to reduce the Qur'an to a science textbook by showing that every new scientific theory or fact is to be found in it.

For example, some have claimed, especially in Turkey, that the *dabbat al-ard* (little moving creature) mentioned in Qur'an 27:82 is the virus that causes AIDS. However, this is a hasty conclusion for several reasons: The Qur'an is silent about this particle's nature; if we accept this assertion, we also must accept other venereal disease-causing bacteria or viruses; and, we cannot know whether new viral diseases and more lethal than AIDS will appear in the future.

The context in which *dabbat al-ard* appears suggests that it will emerge toward the end of this world, when almost no one believes in God. So, we must not show haste in trying to find some type of correspondence between a Qur'anic verse and every new development in science and technology.

Scientific theories are usually like clothes, for both are discarded after a while. Trying to show that every new scientific fact or theory can be found in the Qur'an displays the Muslim world's inferiority complex and makes science more important than the Qur'an. Each Qur'anic verse and expression has a universal content. Therefore, any time-specific interpretation can address only one aspect of that universal content.

Every interpreter, scientist, and saint prefers a particular aspect as a result of his or her spiritual discovery or intuition, personal evidence, or natural disposition. Besides, we accept both Newton's physics and Einstein's physics as science and therefore true. Although in absolute terms both may be false, there certainly must be some truth in both.

Causality is a veil spread by God Almighty over the rapid flux of existence so that we can plan our lives to some degree. This means that Newton's physics and Einstein's physics are only relatively true. In short, while pondering the Qur'anic verses, we should consider the relative truths found in existence and our lives, which are much more numerous than the unchanging absolute truths.

Qur'anic expressions have multiple meanings. For example, consider the verses: *He has let flow forth the two large bodies of water, they meet together, between them is a barrier, which they do not transgress (and so they do not merge)* (55:19-20). These verses indicate all the pairs of "seas" or realms, spiritual and material, figurative and actual, from the realms of Lordship and servanthood to the spheres of necessity and contingency, from this world to the Hereafter (including this visible, corporeal world and all unseen worlds), the Pacific and Atlantic oceans, the Mediterranean and Red seas, salt water and sweet water in the seas and underground, and such large rivers as the Euphrates and Tigris that carry sweet water and salty seas to which they flow. All of these, together with many others, are included in these verses, whether literally or figuratively.

So even if a Qur'anic verse or expression appears to point exactly to an established scientific fact, we should not restrict its meaning to that fact. Rather, we should consider all other possible meanings and interpretations as well.

On the other hand, sometimes the Qur'an does point or allude to specific scientific developments and facts. Being the Divine Revelation that includes anything *green or dry* (6:59), it cannot exclude them. Indeed, it refers to them directly or indirectly, but not in the manner of science and materialistic or naturalistic philosophy.

The Qur'an is not a science textbook that has to expound upon cosmological or scientific matters; rather, it is the eternal interpretation of the Book of the Universe and the interpreter of all natural and other sciences. It comments upon the visible and invisible worlds, and discloses the spiritual treasures of the Divine Beautiful Names in the heavens and Earth. The Qur'an is the key leading to an understanding of the hidden realities behind the events taking place in nature and human life, and is the tongue of the hidden worlds in the manifest world.

The Qur'an is like the sun shining in the spiritual and intellectual sky of Islam. It is the sacred map of the next world; the expounder of the Divine Attributes, Names, and acts; and the educator of humanity that guides us to truth and virtue. It is a book of law and wisdom, worship and prayer, Divine commands and prohibitions. Fully satisfying our spiritual and intellectual needs, it leaves no theological, social, economic, political, or even scientific issue undiscussed, whether in brief or in detail, directly or through allusion or symbols.

The Qur'an considers creation only for the sake of knowing its Creator; science considers creation only for its own sake. The Qur'an addresses humanity; science addresses only those who specialize in it. Since the Qur'an uses creation as evidence and proof to guide us, its evidence must be easily understandable to all of us non-specialists. Guidance requires that relatively unimportant things should be touched on briefly, while subtle points should be discussed as completely as possible through parables and comparisons. So that people are not confused, guidance should not change that which is obvious. If it did, how could we derive any benefit?

Like everything else, science has its source in one of God Almighty's Beautiful Names. The Name All-Healing shines on medicine; geometry and engineering depend on the Names All-Just, All-Shaping, and All-Harmonizing; and philosophy reflects the Name All-Wise. As pointed out above, the Creator refers in the Qur'an to everything that He has allowed us to learn and use for our material and spiritual progress.

The Qur'an's primary aims are to make God Almighty known, to open the way to faith and worship, and to organize our individual and social life so that we may attain perfect happiness in both worlds. To achieve this aim, it refers to things and events, as well as to scientific facts, in proportion to their importance. Thus the Qur'an provides detailed explanations of the pillars of faith, the fundamentals of religion, the foundations of human life, and essentials of worship, but only hints at other relatively less significant things. The meaning of a verse may be compared to a rosebud: it is hidden by successive layers of petals. A new meaning is perceived as each petal unfolds, and people discover one of those meanings according to their capacity and are satisfied with it.

EXAMPLES

Below are some examples that illustrate the Qur'an's allusions to scientific facts and developments.

AGE OF KNOWLEDGE: The Creator, Who is not bound by the human concept of time, informs us that, in a general sense, the future will be the age of knowledge and information, as well as an age of faith and belief:

> We will show them Our manifest signs (proofs) in the horizons of the universe and within their own selves, until it will become manifest to them that this is indeed the truth. Is it not sufficient (as proof) that your Lord is a witness over all things? (41:53)

From the very early days of Islam, Sufis have interpreted this verse as a sign and assurance of the spiritual wisdom for which they strive. But if the verse is read in the context of scientific progress, a progress significantly initiated and advanced by Muslims, the mere fact of the verse will be seen to be a miracle.

Everything within the fold of human thinking and research affirms the Creator's Oneness, as the true nature and interrelationship of microcosm and macrocosm come to be further disclosed and better understood. When we see hundreds of books on this point, we understand that what was Divinely revealed is near at hand. Even now we feel that we shall soon hear and even understand testimonies and praises to God through thousands of nature's tongues:

> The seven heavens and Earth, and all things therein, declare
> His Glory. There is not a thing but celebrates His praise. And
> yet you do not understand how they declare His Glory. Truly
> He is Oft-Forbearing, Most Forgiving. (17:44)

We already understand something of this verse's import. The smallest atoms as well as the largest nebulae speak to us, in the language of their being, of their submission to the One God and so glorify Him. However, those who can listen to and understand this universal praise are very few.

THE FORMATION OF EMBRYO: What the Qur'an reveals about the embryo's formation and developmental phases in the uterus is striking. Consider the following:

> O humanity! If you have a doubt about the Resurrection, (con-
> sider) that We created you out of dust, then out of sperm, then
> out of a leech-like cloth, then out of a lump of flesh, partly
> formed and partly unformed, in order that We may manifest
> (what We will) to you. (22:5)

In another verse, this development is explained in greater detail, and the distinct phases are emphasized more clearly:

> Man We created from a quintessence (of clay). Then We placed
> him as (a drop of) sperm in a place of rest, firmly fixed. Then
> we made the sperm into a clot of congealed blood. Then of that
> clot We made a lump (embryo); then we made out of that lump
> bones and clothed the bones with flesh. Then We developed
> out of it a new (distinct, individual) creature. (23:12-4)

MIRACULOUS PRODUCTION OF MILK: What the Qur'an says about milk and its production is as brilliant as the drink itself, and our understanding of it has brought us great benefits:

> And verily in cattle (too) will you find an instructive sign. From
> what is from their bodies, between excretions and blood, We
> produce, for your drink, milk, pure and agreeable to those who
> drink it. (16:66)

The Qur'an narrates the process in remarkable detail: part-digestion and absorption of what is ingested as food, and then a second process and refinement in the glands. Milk is a wholesome and agreeable source of human nourishment, and yet its owner rejects it as useless.

CREATION IN PAIRS: The Qur'an reveals that all things are created in pairs: *Glory be to God, Who created in pairs all things, of what Earth produces, of themselves, and of which they have no knowledge* (36:36).

Everything that exists has counterpart, whether opposite or complementary. The complementarity of human, animal, and certain plant genders has long been known. But what about the pairs of things of which we have no knowledge? This may refer to a whole range of entities, inanimate as well as animate. In the subtle forces and principles of nature within (and among) animate or inanimate entities, there are many kinds of pairs. All things, as our modern instruments confirm, occur in twos.

The scientific definition of creation in pairs implies "similar opposites." The Qur'an gives three examples:

- Pairs produced by Earth (positron–electron, antiproton–proton, antineutron–neutron), those with different physical and chemical characteristics (metals and non-metals); biologically opposed pairs (male and female plants and animals), and physically opposed pairs.
- Pairs of their selves (man and woman; such personality traits as cruel–compassionate, generous–stingy; and traits that are similar but subject to opposed value judgments, such as hypocrisy–sincerity).
- Pairs about which we do not know.

The discovery of the positron and "parity" (creation in pairs), mentioned by the Qur'an 14 centuries ago, may be regarded as a turning point in contemporary physics.

CREATION OF THE WORLD: The Qur'an recounts, in its own unique idiom, the first creation of the world and of its living inhabitants:

> Do not the unbelievers see that the heavens and Earth were joined together (as a single mass), before We clove them asunder? We made from water every living thing. Will they not then believe? (21:30)

This meaning of this verse is clear, and should not be obscured with hypotheses as to whether the primary material in creation is an ether or a large cloud, a huge nebula or a mass of hot gas, or something else. The Qur'an states that every living thing was created of water. Whether the water itself was caused by gases and vapors rising from the ground, condensing, and then returning as rain to form seas and prepare a suitable environment for life, or by some other process, is relatively unimportant.

The verse explicitly presents the universe as a single miracle of creation. Each thing in it is an integral part of that miracle and contains signs that prove its claim. Everything is interconnected, just like the leaves of a massive tree. They are all different, but resemble each other and are linked to a common root. The verse also emphasizes water's vitality and significance, for it constitutes three-fourths of the body mass of most living creatures.

THE ORBIT OF THE SUN: The sun has a special and significant place. The Qur'an reveals its most important aspects in four words, whose full meaning cannot be rendered easily: *And the sun runs its course* (mustaqarr) *determined for it. That is His decree, the Exalted in Might, the All-Knowing* (36:38).

Given the context, *mustaqarr* may mean a determined orbit, a fixed place of rest or dwelling, a determined route in time. We are told that the sun runs a predetermined course toward a particular point. Our solar system is heading toward the constellation Lyra at an almost inconceivable speed: Every second we come ten miles closer (almost a million miles a day). Our attention is also drawn to the fact that when the sun finishes its appointed task, it will abide by a command and come to rest.

Such is the richness of the Qur'an, which explains many truths in so few words. Here, in only four words, many vague things were clarified at a time when people generally believed that the sun made a daily circuit around Earth.

EXPANSION OF THE UNIVERSE: Another inspiring and eloquent Qur'anic verse concerns the universe's spreading out or expansion in space. This concept is mentioned in only four words: *And the firmament: We constructed it with power and skill, and We are spreading it* (51:47-48).

The verse reveals that the distance between celestial bodies is increasing, which means that the universe is expanding. In 1922, the astronomer Hubble claimed that all galaxies, except the five closest to Earth, are moving further away into space at a speed directly proportional to their distance from Earth. According to him, a galaxy one million light years distant is moving away at a speed of 168 km/year, a galaxy two million light years distant at twice that speed, and so on. Le Maitre, a Belgian mathematician and priest, later proposed and developed the theory that the universe is expanding. No matter how we try to express this reality, whether through Hubble's coefficient or a future theory, the Revelation is unmistakably clear on the reality itself.

LAWS IN NATURE: The Qur'an provides some indication of the invisible operation of various laws as attraction and repulsion, rotation and revolution: *God is He Who raised the heavens without any pillars that you can see* (13:2).

All celestial bodies move in order, balance, and harmony. They are held and supported by invisible pillars, some of which are repulsion or centrifugal forces: *He holds back the sky from falling on Earth, except by His leave* (22:65).

At any moment, the heavens could fall upon Earth. That the All-Mighty does not allow this to happen is yet another instance of the universal obedience to His Word. Modern science explains this as a balance of centripetal and centrifugal forces. What is of far greater importance, however, is that we turn our minds to that obedience and to the Divine Mercy that holds the universe in its reliable motion, rather than deciding to follow Newton's or Einstein's theories about the mechanical and mathematical terms of that obedience.

TRAVEL TO THE MOON: Previously, some Qur'anic commentators thought that traveling to the moon, once considered a very remote possibility, could be found in: *By the moon's fullness! You shall surely travel from stage to stage* (84:18-19).

Earlier commentators took this as a figurative reference to our spiritual life, an ascent from one stage to the next, and from one heaven to another. Others interpreted it as referring to change in general, from one state to another. Later interpreters gave ambiguous meanings, because the literal meaning did not agree with their beliefs about traveling such distances. But in fact, the more appropriate sense of the words following the oath "By the moon!," given the verse's immediate context, is that of really traveling to the moon, whether literally or figuratively.

THE SHAPE OF THE EARTH: The Qur'anic description of Earth's geographical shape and change in that shape are particularly interesting: *Do they not see how We gradually shrink the land from its outlying borders? Is it then they who will be victors?* (21:44).

The reference to shrinking could relate to the now-known fact that Earth is compressed at the poles, rather than to the erosion of mountains by wind and rain, of coastal areas by the sea, or of the gradual desertification of agricultural land.

At a time when people generally believed that Earth was flat and stationary, the Qur'an explicitly and implicitly revealed that it is round. More unexpectedly still, it also says that its precise shape is more like an ostrich egg than a sphere: *After that He shaped Earth like an egg, whence He caused to spring forth the water thereof, and the pasture thereof* (79:30-32).

The verb *daha'* means "to shape like an egg," and its derived noun *da'hia* is still used to mean "an egg." As this scientific fact may have appeared incorrect to scientists living before the advent of modern science, some interpreters misunderstood the word's meaning. They understood it as "stretched out," perhaps fearing that its literal meaning might be difficult to understand and thus mislead people. Modern scientific instruments recently established that Earth is shaped more like an egg than a perfect sphere, and that there is a slight flattening around the poles as well as a slight curving around the equator.

PROPORTIONATE GRAVITATIONAL ATTRACTION: In: *Then He turned to Heaven when it was smoke, and said to it and to Earth: "Come willingly or unwillingly." They said: "We come willingly"* (40:11), the Qur'an indicates that such cooperation is difficult. We know that the atmosphere's molecules and atoms try to escape into space, while Earth tries to attract and capture them. But for there to be an atmosphere, the motions leading to the molecules' escape must be counterbalanced by Earth's gravitational attraction.

This condition is almost impossible to fulfill. From the standpoint of geophysics, these conditions require that three important balances be preserved: atmospheric temperature, Earth's proportionate gravitational attraction, and the non-violation of this balance by various radiant energies arriving from space. The Qur'an expresses these facts in the verse mentioned above. That such almost impossible conditions are fulfilled only by God's Power is indicated in: *They said: "We come willingly."*

THE PLANETS' SPHERICAL SHAPE AND ROTATIONS: These are indicated in: *He is the Lord of the heavens and Earth, and all that lies between them; He is the Lord of the easts* (37:15), for the concept of *the easts* introduces infinite dimensions and differs for each location on Earth. A point on Earth is in the east with respect to its western regions. Therefore the concept of *east* differs at every point on Earth, and these form an ensemble of *easts*. Besides, there are 180 points of sunrise, which means that the sun rises at one place for only 2 days in the year and thus there are 180 *easts*. And so this verse also indicates meridians, infinite dimensions, space's relativity, the planets' spherical shape, and Earth's rotation.

A BARRIER BETWEEN TWO SEAS: French scientist Jacques Cousteau[23] discovered that the Mediterranean Sea and the Atlantic Ocean have different chemical and biological constitutions. After conducting undersea investigations at the Straits of Gibraltar to explain this phenomenon, he concluded that "unexpected fresh water springs issue from the Southern and Northern coasts of Gibraltar. These water sprouts gush forth towards each other at angle of 45°, forming a reciprocal dam like the teeth of a comb. Due to this fact, the Mediterranean and the Atlantic Ocean cannot intermingle." When shown the verse: *He has let flow forth the two large bodies of water, they meet together, between them is a barrier, which they do not transgress (and so they do not merge)* (55:19-20), Cousteau was amazed.

This verse further draws our attention to the plankton composition of the seas, and to the flora and fish distributions that change with variations in temperature. Many other Qur'anic verses shed light upon scientific facts, and every person is invited to study them: *We made the Qur'an easy for reflection and study. Will anybody study and reflect?* (54:17).

A day will come when *We will show them Our manifest signs (proofs) in the horizons of the universe and within their own selves, until it will become manifest to them that this is indeed the truth.* (41:53). In the future humanity will concentrate more on science, and the Qur'an (the universe's counterpart in letters and the realm in which God's Names are manifested) will prove itself to be God's Revelation.

SCIENTIFIC DEVELOPMENTS CONNECTED WITH CERTAIN HISTORICAL EVENTS: Consider the following examples that allude to trains and electricity:

> Down with the makers of the trench of the fuel-fed fire! When they sat by it, and were themselves the witnesses of what they did to the believers. They ill-treated them for no other reason than that they believed in God, the Mighty, the All-Praised One. (85:4-8)

Likewise, ... in the loaded fleet. And We have created for them the like thereof whereon they ride. (36:41-42)

Verses like these point to trains, while one of the many meanings and connotations that can be found in the following verse alludes to electricity:

God is the Light of the heavens and Earth. The parable of His Light is as a niche wherein is a lamp, the lamp is in a glass. The glass is, as it were, a shining star. Kindled from a blessed tree, an olive, neither of the East nor of the West, whose oil would almost glow forth (of itself) though no fire touched it: Light upon light. God guides to His Light whom He wills. (24:35)

The Qur'an also hints of technological advances and marks their final development by mentioning the Prophets' miracles.

God Almighty sent Prophets to human communities as leaders and vanguards of spiritual and moral progress. He also endowed them with certain wonders and miracles, made them masters and forerunners of humanity's material progress, and commanded humanity to follow them absolutely.

The Qur'an encourages people to benefit from the Prophets' spiritual and moral perfections by mentioning them, and urges people to achieve through science what the Prophets showed to humanity in their miracles. As was the case with spiritual and moral attainments, material attainments and wonders were given to humanity as gifts by means of Prophetic miracles. For example, Noah built the first ship and Joseph made the first clock. Thus both of these are Prophetic miracles given to humanity. This is why so many guilds have adopted a Prophet as a patron or originator of their craft: sailors have Noah, watchmakers have Joseph, and tailors have Enoch.

Since truth-seeking scholars and the science of eloquence have agreed that each Qur'anic verse contains guidance and instruction, those verses (which are the most brilliant) concerning these miracles should not be taken as historical events only, but as containing numerous meanings for guidance. By mentioning these miracles, the Qur'an shows the ultimate goal of scientific and technological developments, specifies their final aims, and urges humanity to pursue those aims. Just as the past is the field for the future's seeds and a mirror to its potential, the future is the time to reap the harvest of the past life and a mirror to the actual situation. Out of many examples, I give only a few:

TRAVELLING IN THE AIR: The verse: *And to Solomon (We subjugated) the wind; its morning course was a month's journey, and its evening course was a month's journey* (34:12) mentions one of Solomon's miracles. It tells us that: "Solomon covered the distance of 2 months walk in two strides by flying through the air." Suggesting that travel by air is possible, it is telling humanity to learn how to do this and then to do it. Almighty God also is saying that "One of My servants did not obey his carnal desires, and so I mounted him on the air. If you give up laziness and benefit properly from certain of My laws in nature, you will be able to do this as well."

CENTRIFUGE AND ARTESIAN WELLS:

> When Moses asked for water for his people, We said: "Strike the rock with your staff." Then gushed forth therefrom 12 springs (so that) each tribe knew their drinking place. (2:60)

This verse indicates that simple tools enable one to benefit from underground treasuries of Mercy. Water may be drawn out in places that are as hard as rock with a simple tool. In other words: "Since you can find Mercy's finest blessing—water—with a staff-like device, strive to find it." Through this verse, God Almighty suggests: "I gave a staff to one of My servants who relied on Me. With it, he draws forth water from wherever he wishes. If you rely on My laws of Mercy, you can obtain a similar device. So, come and do so."

One important result of scientific progress is the invention of devices that cause water to well up at most of the places where they are applied. The verse points to further goals and limits beyond that, just as the previous one specified further attainments far ahead of today's airplanes.

A CURE FOR EVERY ILLNESS: The verse: *I also heal the blind and the leper, and bring to life the dead, by the leave of God* (3:49) is about one of Jesus' miracles. It alludes to and encourages the highest level of healing with which the Lord endowed him, and suggests: "Even the most chronic ailments have a cure. So do not despair, O children of Adam. Rather, search for it and you will find it. It might even give a temporary tinge of life to death."

By this verse God Almighty means: "One of My servants renounced the world for My sake, and so I gave him two gifts: the remedy for spiritual ailments and the cure for physical sicknesses. Dead hearts were quickened through the light of guidance, and those people who were at death's door because of their illness were healed through his breath and cure. You may find the cure for all illnesses in My pharmacy in nature, where I attached many important purposes to each thing. If you search for it diligently, surely you will find it." This verse marks the final point of medical progress, a point far ahead of the present level, and urges humanity toward it.

Many other Qur'anic verses allude to the ultimate goals of scientific progress, as do some of the Prophetic Traditions. For example, the reliable sources of Tradition record the Prophet's prediction that one day a single pomegranate would be enough for as many as 20 people and that its rind would provide shade for them. He also prophesied that the wheat produced in an area the size of a house's balcony would be enough to feed a family for a year.[24]

- The verse: *Said he who possessed some knowledge of the Book: "I will bring it (the throne of the Queen of Sheba) to you (to Solomon in Jerusalem) in the twinkling of your eye"* (27:40), foretells that one day images or even physical items will be transmitted instantly through knowledge of the Divine Book of the Universe, just as those who have knowledge of the Book of Divine Revelation can bring things from a long distance in the blink of an eye.

- The Qur'an symbolically informs us that it might be possible to identify a murderer by some cells taken from his body at the time of death: A murderer was revealed in the time of Moses by smiting the slain man with part of a cow that God Almighty ordered the Children of Israel to slaughter (2:67-73).

- As a last example, consider what the Qur'an says about the sun and the moon: *We have made the night and the day as two signs; the sign of the night We have obscured, while the sign of the day We have made to enlighten you* (17:12).

  According to Ibn 'Abbas, the *sign of the night* refers to the moon, and the *sign of the day* to the sun. Therefore, from *the sign of the night We have obscured*, we understand that the moon once emitted light just as the sun does, and that for some reason God took away its light, causing it to darken or become obscured. While the verse accurately recounts the moon's past, it also points to the future destiny of other heavenly bodies.

Many other verses are related to what we now call scientific facts. Their existence indicates that our quest for knowledge is a portion of Divine Mercy graciously bestowed by our Creator. Indeed, Divine Mercy is one of the Qur'an's names for itself. All the truth and knowledge that it contains is beyond our ability to recount or even to hold in our mind.

We must remember, however, that while the Qur'an alludes to many scientific truths, it is not a textbook of science or scientific explanations. Rather it is, and has always been understood by believers to be, the book of guidance that teaches us the way to right belief and right action so that we may be worthy of Divine Mercy and Forgiveness. It is our responsibility to ensure that the pursuit of scientific and other kinds of knowledge is conducted in the light of the Qur'an, which so encourages and supports it.

Such an approach results in knowledge that will not engender arrogance and self-pride, for such feelings lead to mental desolation and human degradation, not to mention the degradation of Earth, our temporary home and Divinely given trust.

WHY WE REFER TO SCIENCE AND SCIENTIFIC FACTS

We refer to science and scientific facts when explaining Islam because some people only accept scientific facts. Materialists and both non- and anti-religious people have sought to exploit science to defy religion and give their ideas more prestige than they deserve. Through this approach, they have misled and corrupted the minds of many people. Therefore, we must learn how to talk with them in their own terminology to prove that science and technology do not contradict Islam. We have to turn their arguments against them by evaluating them and then using them to guide people to the right way.

Such an approach is entirely permissible, for how can we dispute what such people say if we are not well-versed in their facts and ideas? The Qur'an urges us to reflect and study, to observe the stars and galaxies. They impress upon us the Magnificence of the Creator, exhort us to wander among people, and direct our attention to the miraculous nature of our organs and physical creation.

From atoms to the largest beings, from the first human being's appearance on Earth until our final departure, the Qur'an places all creation before our eyes. Touching upon a multitude of facts, it tells us that *those who truly fear God, among His servants, are those who have knowledge* (35:28), and so encourages us to seek knowledge, to reflect and research. However, we must never forget that all such activities must comply with the spirit of the Qur'an. Otherwise, even though we claim to be following its advice and command, actually we will be moving away from it.

Science and its facts can and should be used to explain Islamic facts. But if we use them to show off our knowledge, whatever we say cannot influence our audience in the right way, if at all.

Bright and persuasive words and arguments lose their effectiveness if we have the wrong intention: they get as far as the listeners' ear-drums and no further. Similarly, if our arguments seek to silence others instead of persuading them, we actually will block their way to a correct understanding. Our effort will fail, and our goals will remain unachieved.

However, if we try to persuade with a full and proper sincerity, even those who need such arguments to believe will receive their portion and benefit. Sometimes a sincere argument may be far more beneficial than one in which you spoke rather more freely and eloquently. Our primary aim when introducing science and scientific facts, in accordance with our audience's level of understanding, must be to win the pleasure of God.

Science cannot be regarded as superior to religion, and substantial Islamic issues cannot use science or modern scientific facts to justify or reinforce religion's credibility. If we adopt such techniques, we are proclaiming that we have doubts about the truths of Islam and need science to support them. In addition, we cannot accept science or scientific facts as absolute. Making science the decisive criteria for the Qur'an's authenticity or Divine origin, thereby placing science over the Qur'an, is absurd, abhorrent, and completely impermissible. Such arguments and allusions to science have, at best, a secondary and supportive use. Their only possible value is that they might open a door onto a way that certain people simply would not know exists.

Science is to be used to awaken or stir some minds that otherwise might remain asleep or unmoved. It is like a feather duster used to brush the dust off the truth and the desire for truth, which lie hidden in unstirred consciences. If we begin by saying that science is absolute, we shall end up seeking to fit the Qur'an and Hadith to it. The result of such an undertaking can only be doubt and confusion especially when we cannot reconcile the Qur'an and Hadith with some present assertions of science that may be falsified in the future.

Our position must be clear: The Qur'an and Hadith are true and absolute. Science and scientific facts are true (or false) only to the degree that they agree (or disagree) with these sources. Even definitely established scientific facts cannot be pillars to uphold the truths of faith; rather, they can be accepted only as instruments giving us ideas or triggering our reflection on God, Who establishes the truths of faith in our conscience. To expect that this does or even could take place through science is a grave error, for faith comes only by Divine guidance.

Anyone who fails to grasp this has fallen into an error from which it is hard to recover. Such people look for and gather evidence from the universe and, trying to make it speak eloquently in the Name of God, remain unconscious servants to nature and nature worshippers. They study and speak of flowers, of the verdancy and spring of nature, but not the least greenness or bud of faith sprouts in their conscience. They may never even feel the existence of God within their consciousness. In appearance they do not worship nature, but in reality that is what they are doing.

A man or a woman is a believer *(mu'min)* owing to the faith in his or her heart, not to the great amount of knowledge in his or her head. After we have understood as much as we can about the objective and subjective evidence we have gathered, we must break our dependence on the outer circumstances, qualities, and conditions of such evidence. Only by doing this will we be able to make any spiritual progress. When we abandon this dependence and follow our heart and conscience within the Qur'an's light and guidance, then, if God wills, we will find the enlightenment for which we are looking. As the German philosopher Immanuel Kant once said: "I felt the need to leave behind all the books I have read in order to believe in God."

Undoubtedly, the grand Book of the Universe and the book of humanity's true nature (the Qur'an), as well as their commentaries, have their proper place and significance. But after we use them, we should put them aside and live with our faith, as it were, face to face. This might sound rather abstract to those who have not gone deep into the experience of faith and conscience. But for those whose nights are bright with devotion, and who acquire wings through their longing to aspire to their Lord, the meaning is clear.

QUESTION: Why have Muslims not developed science and discovered such Qur'anic truths? Why does the West dominate them?

ANSWER: To the extent that time and the prevalent conditions allowed them to, Muslims discovered the Qur'an's truths and, obeying its injunctions, founded a magnificent civilization that lasted for many centuries.

A typical example: While explaining the meaning of: *We send the wind fertilizing, and cause water to descend from the sky, and give it you to drink* (15:22), Ibn Jarir al-Tabari (839-923) writes about how the winds fertilize clouds so that rain may form. The verse clearly mentions the winds fertilizing clouds because it is about the formation of rain. Scientists recently discovered that clouds also are charged with electricity and that rain forms only when positive and negative poles in clouds form a circuit.

In his *Al-Bahr al-Muhit*, Abu Hayyan al-Andalusi records from Abu Ja'far ibn al-Zubayr that, based upon

> Alif Lam Mim. The Romans have been defeated in the nearer land, and they, after their defeat, will be victorious within 9 years—God's is the command in the former case and in the latter—and in that day believers will rejoice in God's help to victory. He helps to victory whom He wills. He is the Mighty, the Merciful. (30:1-5)

Abu al-Hakim ibn Barrajan deduced the exact day, month, and year when the Muslims would recapture Jerusalem from the Crusaders (1187) long before they did so.

Islam ruled two-thirds of the old civilized world for at least 11 centuries. During its 1,400-year existence, it has confronted continual onslaughts from the East and the West—and yet it maintained its superiority until the eighteenth century! However, only when the Muslims' own moral and spiritual decay, laziness, and negligence of what was going on around them were added to these attacks did the magnificence and supremacy of Islamic civilization began to decline, until it finally collapsed soon after World War I. Military victories and a sense of superiority had persuaded Muslims to rest on their laurels and neglect further scientific research. They abandoned themselves to living their own lives and reciting the Qur'an without studying its deeper meanings.

Meanwhile, the West made great scientific and technological progress. These were borrowed from Islamic civilization. As science is, in reality, no more than the languages of the Divine Book of Creation and an aspect of religion, whoever does not study this book and benefit from it loses in this life. Such negligence was one of the main reasons why Europe conquered the Muslim world.

Modern materialistic civilization cannot endure for long, because it is materialistic and unable to satisfy our perennial needs. Such Western sociologists as Oswald Spengler have predicted its collapse, as it is against basic human nature and values. Either it will abandon itself to its inevitable decay or equip itself with Islam's creeds, moral and spiritual values, and socioeconomic principles. In other words, Muslims will rediscover that science and religion are, in essence, two aspects of the same reality. Once again they will know that being Muslim means, first of all, to represent Islam's beauties in practical life. The luminous world of the future will be founded upon the firm foundations of Islamic morality, spirituality, and its other principles.

CAUSALITY AND THE QUR'ANIC WORLDVIEW

Yamine Mermer

The universe has been made in the form of an intelligible book so that its Author can be known. The book addresses humanity and calls upon all people to read it and respond with worship and thanksgiving to its Author's Will. Humanity attains this level by uncovering, through scientific study, the order displayed in the Book of the Universe as well as its inhabitants' functioning.

The universe is neither passive nor neutral. We cannot interpret it as we wish, for there is only one correct way of looking at it, one universal worldview common to humanity. The Creator teaches this to us through the Qur'an and the Book of the Universe. This does not mean that the Qur'anic worldview rejects the idea that the perception of the world differs from one person to another. Rather, it allows for plurality within unity so that a universal dialogue is possible. This worldview contains no fragmentation or conflict, but only harmony, assistance, peace, and compassion.

The materialist scientific worldview is based on radical fragmentation, for its adherents consider nature to be a mechanism with no inherent value and meaning. It isolates an object by severing its connections with the rest of the world so that it can be studied within its immediate environment. It does this despite the fact that our perception of ourselves tells us that we are meaningful and part of the whole universe, and that everything must have a meaning and be part of the universe. Materialist science has left the subject—humanity—out of the universe and, insofar as this science is taking over, people feel that they have no place in this world. Such a view isolates people from each other and deprives their lives of meaning, except in a very limited, egoistic sense. Thus people are alienated from their surrounding environments and from themselves.

Modern physics has shown this mechanistic view to be an incoherent description of nature. Developments in modern physics, which have shattered all the principal concepts of classical physics, call for a radical revision of our concept of reality. Many concepts, such as the causal nature of physical phenomena and the ideal of an objective description of nature, changed with the advent of new theories in modern science: quantum, relativity, and, more recently, chaos theory.

However, these changes took place only on a mathematical level and have not been matched by parallel changes in the worldview of science, for scientists only are interested in developing mathematical formulations of the behavior of physical phenomena. Such a goal is not regarded merely for its technical utility; rather, most scientists believe that predictions of this kind are the ultimate reason for knowledge and that our concept of reality is of little or no importance. However, it is clear that our concept of reality has a tremendous effect on how we behave in relation to nature and other people, and also on the meaning life has for us as individuals. Therefore, we cannot dispense with a worldview.

This contemporary scientific attitude actually contradicts modern science. Classically, it was thought that science could describe and explain everything in the world *objectively* (as it actually is in reality) and that the *observer* (the scientist) could describe the world through judgment-free mathematical models. However, discoveries in modern physics point toward the unity of all things, an unbroken wholeness that denies the classical fragmentation of the world into separate and independent parts. In quantum theory, every particle is linked to, and cannot be isolated from, the rest of the universe. This oneness of the universe includes human beings as well. Quantum theory, together with abolishing the notion of fundamentally separate objects, has replaced the *neutral observer* with the *participator*. Modern science therefore restores humanity to its central position. It ends the notion of a neutral and objective description of nature and thus of impartial and objective science.

Up to the present, materialist science has been based on a deterministic, causal view of the world. Although the latest theories (e.g., quantum and chaos) are leading to a worldview that has no place for fragmentation and determinism, materialist scientists insist upon following the fragmented and causal approach. They do so because, as believers in causality, they are reductionists and well aware that their materialist worldview is collapsing. They understand, theoretically, that explaining one thing requires that they know its connections to all other things. This is obviously impossible, because these connections extend in time and in space beyond human capacities. Moreover, they are infinite and cannot be embraced by human beings, as human beings are parts of those connections.

Materialist scientists understand that the universe's unity points to an Absolute Creator, for the things that we study do not bear meanings limited to themselves but testify to their Creator's Absoluteness. But they insist on denying the Absolute Creator in order to claim that their studies produce knowledge. And because their scientific method is based on causality, which cannot accommodate such a unity, they ignore that unity and compartmentalize the universe so that they can study each compartment as the product of a limited number of causes. This allows them to pretend the universe has no Creator and that its meaning is limited to what they tell us about it. Thus, they claim that their science is the source of knowledge.

The conceptual foundations of modern physics have been quite controversial. The mechanistic model of reality is not appropriate to modern science. Scientists avoid this issue by adopting the attitude that the paradoxes and contradictions found in their science are inherent in nature, thus implying that those paradoxes and contradictions have nothing to do with their inadequate worldview.

But how one can apply reductionist scientific reasoning to the inseparable universe? Scientists and philosophers have discussed this matter at great length, but do not seem to have realized yet that the nature of the materialistic approach to scientific reasoning is incompatible with the universe's unity. Therefore, either that approach to scientific reasoning or the concept of the universe's unity has to be reconsidered.

No one disputes the fact that the universe is an inseparable whole. Indeed, the unity observed within it and within humanity is so clear that it cannot be denied. Therefore the materialistic approach to the scientific method has to be reconsidered. This method reduces every thing to fragments and then attributes each fragment to causes, even though all things are interconnected and interdependent. For this reason, nothing can be attributed to causes, regardless of size, for causes are themselves transient and contingent. Since whatever is responsible for one thing must be responsible for all things, we cannot have one thing without the whole.

Why can we ascribe a thing to its antecedents in time but not to its neighbors in space? Why should a thing be able to produce another thing just because it happened before? Modern scientists know that space and time are fully equivalent and unified into a four-dimensional continuum in which *here* and *there*, as well as *before* and *after*, are relative. In this four-dimensional space, the temporal sequence is converted into a simultaneous coexistence, the side-by side existence of all things. Thus causality appears to be an idea limited to a prejudiced experience of the world.

Causality leads to the vicious chain of cause and effect, for each cause is also an effect. Also, the effect is totally different from the cause. Things and effects are usually so full of art and beneficial purposes that, let alone their simple immediate causes, even if all causes gathered together they could not produce one single thing.

In short, in order for a cause to produce an effect, it has to be able to produce the whole universe in which that effect takes place, for that effect cannot exist without the whole universe. They cannot exist separately. Causality is therefore the antitheses of "There is no god but God," the core of the Qur'anic worldview. Materialist scientists imagine powerless, dependent, and ignorant causes to be responsible for the existence of beings and things, and thus imagine that they possess absolute qualities. In this way, they imply (and tacitly believe) that each cause possesses qualities that can be attributed only to God.

However, the latest discoveries of modern science, among the universe's unity and the inseparability of its parts, exclude the possibility of all such materialistic explanations. They demonstrate that all entities, whether in nature or in the laws and causes attributed to them, are devoid of power and knowledge because they are contingent, transient, and dependent. But the properties attributed to any such entity must include such infinite qualities as absolute power and knowledge.

This shows that causality is by no means necessarily linked with *objective* study or *neutral* scientific investigation. It is no more than an irrational and non-sensical personal opinion. Nevertheless, there is still a widespread conviction that science can do without a Creator. While this seemed possible in classical physics, it is untenable in quantum mechanics. Physics is full of examples of ingenuity and subtlety that exclude the causal interpretation and make known the All-Powerful, All-Knowing One. A few illustrations, I hope, will suffice to convince us that the universe and all of its contents are His products.

The idea that the universe began with a "Big Bang" is rather paradoxical. Of nature's four forces, only gravity acts systematically on a cosmic scale, and in our experience gravity is attractive, a pulling force. But the explosion marking the universe's creation required a powerful pushing force to set it on its still-continuing path of expansion. It is puzzling that the expanding universe is dominated by the force of gravity, which is contracting instead of expanding. Careful measurements show that the rate of expansion has been "very fine-tuned" to fall on this narrow line between two catastrophes: a little slower and the cosmos would collapse, a little faster and the cosmic material long ago would have dispersed completely.

Materialist scientists see that such a precisely calculated explosion requires infinite power and knowledge, and yet deny the act of creation. Therefore they are compelled to say: "It just happened; it must be accepted as a special initial condition." The initial condition, however, had to be very special indeed. And the rate of expansion is only one of countless cosmic miracles. But in their misguidance, they imagine those miracles of the Absolute Power to be "remarkable" coincidences and imply that the universe is a random accident. In short, the most fundamental theory of recent modern science is totally compatible with the concept of the Absolute Creator—but not with causality. Thus the need for God, the Causer of causes, enters science in a fundamental way.

Classically, it is believed that a measurement performed in one place cannot instantaneously affect a particle in another and very distant place. This is based on the assumption that interactions between systems tend to decline with distance, since causality holds that a cause has to be in the immediate vicinity of its effect. Otherwise how can two particles several meters—let alone light years—apart influence each other's position and motion?

In contrast, quantum mechanics predicts a greater degree of correlation, as though the two particles cooperate by telepathy. This forces us to ask: How can this remarkable degree of cooperation between different parts of the universe that have never been in communication with each other be explained without mentioning their Creator? How can they achieve this miracle? Divine Unity is obviously the only reasonable, consistent, and acceptable—to the point of being necessary—explanation of this miracle and indeed of the universe, its contents, and humanity.

Materialists are caught in a paradox here, for causality cannot explain such cooperation. But for believers in God, this beautiful aspect of His Unity envisions a universal coherence and
points to all-encompassing principles running throughout the
cosmos.

When we break the vicious chain of cause and effect, the
meaningless world of materialism gives way to a world illumined
with meaning and purpose. The universe becomes like a vast book
addressing humanity and making its Author known so that its readers can take lessons, constantly increase in knowledge of their
Maker, and strengthen their belief and certainty in the fundamentals of faith.

In short, everything is full of art and is being renewed constantly, and both the cause of each thing and its effect are created. In order to exist, each thing must possess infinite power and
knowledge. Thus there must exist a Possessor of Absolute Power
and Knowledge Who directly creates the cause and the effect,
which together demonstrate their Maker's Attributes. They proclaim the Divine Power and Perfection through their own pow-
erlessness and deficiency, and announce: "There is no god but
God."

Just as the universe points to this truth of Divine Unity, so
does the universe's Owner teach us this truth in His revealed
sacred books.[1] The phrase "There is no god but God" is the fundamental Revelation and is confirmed by the testimony of beings.
It is the key to the Qur'an, a key that makes it possible to understand the riddle of the universe's creation, a riddle that has reduced
materialist science and philosophy to impotence. The path of Unity
is the path of Revelation. Only this path shows humanity its
Master and Owner and causes us to recognize our True Object
of Worship Who possesses an absolute power that will fulfill all
of our needs.

The Qur'an is the only source that teaches us that the universe and its inhabitants do not bear a meaning limited to themselves but testify to their Maker's Unity. It teaches what the uni-

verse is and what duties it is performing. This is why Muslims should study the universe and see that all beings, through their order, mutual relationship and duties, refute the false claims of materialist and atheistic reasoning by affirming that they are nothing but the property and creatures of a Single Creator. Each rejects the false notions of chance and causality, and ascribes all other beings to its own Creator. Each is a proof that the Creator has no partners. Indeed, when the Creator's Unity is known and understood correctly, it becomes clear that there is no reason why causes should possess any power. Therefore it is impossible for them to be partners of the Creator. This causes Muslim scientists to say, through their investigations and discoveries: "There is no god but God, alone and without partner."

The universe is a document to be read by believers. Believing in God is, as the Qur'an informs us, to assent with one's heart to the Creator with all of His Attributes supported by the testimony of the universe. The true affirmation of God's Unity is a judgment, a confirmation, an assent and acceptance that can find its Owner present with all things. It sees in all things a path leading to its Owner, and regards nothing as an obstacle to His presence. If this were not the case, it would be necessary to tear and cast aside the universe in order to find Him, and that is impossible for us.

The universe is not the property of materialistic science, which has used the universe in a destructive way precisely because it has been unable to discover its meaning. There is no dichotomy between true science and Revelation. Rather, true human progress and happiness can be achieved only in the way of the Qur'an. All scientific and technological advances are merely the uncovering of the way the universe was created. When the universe is seen to be a vast and meaningful unified book describing its Author and its inhabitants as signs of their Creator, all of these discoveries and advances reinforce belief rather than cause doubt and bewilderment.

The most serious disease now afflicting humanity in our search for happiness and the meaning of life is to regard science, the study of the created world, as separate from and irreconcilable with Revelation, the Word of the Creator. But as we learn to heed the universe and our senses, rather than the materialist scientists, we will notice the contradictions of their scientific reasoning. More and more people are beginning to realize that [materialist] scientific reasoning is no longer valid. Faced with beauty, awesomeness, and purpose, attempts to explain creation with causality are becoming increasingly untenable. Upon reaching this point, they will feel the need and importance for true science and knowledge that yield knowledge and belief in God.

WHAT A FALLING STONE MEANS

Salih Adem

The laws of physics are mathematical expressions of how the universe operates. The events taking place in the universe, as well as the relations between them and the laws "governing" the universe, have drawn the attention of people since ancient times.

Scientists have tried to explain whatever takes place in the universe, such as the movements of heavenly objects, tides, and the floating of ships on water. However, according to ancient Greek thinkers, scientists had to concentrate on humanity rather than the natural world. They believed that natural phenomena and the laws governing them could be explained through such mental operations as deduction and analogical reasoning.

The Qur'an calls humanity's attention to the Divine manifestations on creatures (e.g., the honeybee, ant, gnat, and spider) and invites people to reflect on and study such phenomena as the movement of air, the alternation of day and night and the seasons, and the movements of heavenly bodies. The importance given by the Qur'an to the study of natural events inspired Muslim scientists to pursue observation and experimentation long before these came into use in Europe.

Science passed to Europe through the Crusades, the universities in al-Andalus (Muslim Spain) and Sicily, and translations of Arabic texts. Science was the main factor behind the European Renaissance. Building on (but never openly acknowledging) the work of Muslim scientists, European scientists led the way in giving birth to modern science. Until correct conclusions were reached about phenomena through observation and experimental methods, the assertions of ancient Greek philosophers had been accepted as the basic laws of nature. For example, since Aristotle's time people had believed that the speed of an object's falling is proportionate to its weight. However, Galileo and Newton conducted experiments that proved this to be false. They discovered that so long as the air's resistance is negligible in proportion to the object's weight and its vertical cross-sectional area, an object's unhindered movement on Earth is not dependent upon its mass. In other words, objects of different weights dropped from the same point reach Earth at the same time.

Such developments in physics led scientists to approve of observation and experimentation as basic rules in establishing natural facts. Scientists were tasked with discovering the laws and basic truths prevalent in the universe through these two empirical methods, while philosophers were to reflect and comment upon them. In other words, reaching true conclusions about the universe and the events taking place in it means discarding all preconceptions, studying nature through empirical methods, and then commenting up on natural events and the relations between them.

To have a clearer understanding of modern science and what it can tell us about the universe, consider the law of general gravity, an undeniably established scientific fact. Various observations and experiments have shown that any two objects attract each other or exert force upon each other proportionately to their masses and in inverse proportion to the square of the distance between them.

The force of attraction (gravity) is the force in effect in such events as a falling object and Earth's revolving around the sun. Science presents gravity as if it were the cause of such events. However, what we call the force of gravitation is only a notion we use to explain those events. By this we mean that that there is an attraction observed between objects, and that we try to explain it by giving it a particular name, such as the law or force of gravitation, and then think that we have explained the event of attraction.

Science does not know the nature of this force. But, starting from the assertion that scientists have explained many events whose causes were unknown in the past, science claims that what it cannot explain now will become, at some point in the future, explainable. Nevertheless, science cannot explain the real cause of all events in the universe. All it can do is, starting from the recurrence of an event under the same conditions, to make a generalization and call it a law. It then asserts that the same event will take place again and again under the same conditions. For example, after observing the falling of objects thrown into the air, it makes a generalization that all objects thrown into the air will fall and expresses this event of falling by a mathematical formula.

Let's consider how science works to calculate and state beforehand the length of time it will take for an object thrown into the air with a certain force and at a certain angle to fall, and at what distance it will fall. Since events occur in a cause-and-effect series, knowing what effect or event will occur in the next step does not require an understanding of why it occurs in that way. Therefore, although we suppose that the law of gravity will be understood as, say, dependent upon an exchange between certain particles or the obliquity of spatial time, scientific methods will be unable to explain why such an exchange takes place, why the spatial time becomes oblique, or why that exchange or obliquity occurs according to certain mathematical formulations that cause objects to attract each other.

In addition to the fact that the reason for this attraction remains unknown, it is also a mystery (and a wonder) that such attraction takes place according to a mathematical formula. Due to our familiarity with the events taking place in nature, we ignore the important fact that every thing and event in nature is a miracle. In order to see why the event of gravitation is a dazzling miracle, we should consider it more closely:

Consider the falling of a stone dropped (and then allowed to fall unhindered) from a certain high point. Left unhindered, that stone will realize a certain trajectory as the result of gravity affecting it. It will move faster and faster until it finally hits the ground. How the stone will accelerate, how long it will take it to reach the ground, and how it will move at every second of its trajectory depends upon the stone's distance from Earth's center, Earth's mass, and the constant of gravity. Thus the stone does not move at random; rather, each movement during its fall is calculable by mathematical formulas. This is an extremely regular movement.

From this, we inevitably conclude that if the stone does this movement of falling by itself, without an agent directing or determining its trajectory, the stone must know accurately the constant of gravity, Earth's mass, its distance from Earth's center at each moment of its trajectory, and then move in conformity with that knowledge. No rational person will say that the stone can determine its own trajectory, which is simple in appearance but extremely complex in reality.

Indeed, the falling of a stone is so complex a movement that during it all the objects in the universe, every thing with a certain mass, exerts a certain force of attraction upon it. Thus the stone moves under the influence of those forces.[1] That is, in order to determine its trajectory, the stone must know the exact distance between itself and each of about 1080 particles in the universe, calculate accurately at each moment of its trajectory the force of the attraction exerted on it by each particle according to the mathematical formula of gravity—a force that changes every moment—and focus all those forces on a single point in consideration of the direction of each.

Let alone a stone, even the most advanced and largest computer imaginable could not accomplish this, for the position of each particle, with respect to the stone, changes at every moment during its fall. Thus, even the apparently most simple movement in the universe, such as the falling of a stone, requires a comprehensive knowledge and mastery of an infinite number of interrelated processes.

Since any event taking place in any part of the universe is connected with each particle in the universe and with the universe itself, only one who has a perfect knowledge of and can see each particle and the universe can determine and direct all of the movements in the universe. Also, since the law of gravity and all other physical laws are the same and uniform throughout the universe, one who makes these laws operative must be an absolutely powerful one who dominates each and every thing therein. Otherwise, each atom in the universe must have an eye that sees the whole universe at the same time and knows the position, mass, electrical charge—in short, all physical features—of each particle in the universe, be aware of all the physical laws, and obey the laws that it originated.

Every event and thing in the universe is interrelated to every other, and whatever occurs therein happens according to certain laws. Therefore, it is impossible for even the smallest and apparently most insignificant event to take place in the absence of one having an absolute, perfect knowledge of the universe and all of its particles, as well as having an absolute power governing it. Said Nursi[2] expresses this fact as follows:

> If the existence and operation of the universe is not attributed
> to God Almighty; then it requires admitting that each particle
> has the attributes of the Necessarily Existent Being, and that
> each particle should both dominate and be dominated by all
> other particles. Again, each particle should have an all-encom-
> passing will and knowledge, for the existence of a single thing
> is dependent on all things and one who does not own the uni-
> verse cannot rule a single particle.

After explaining how complex a phenomenon gravitation is, we can go a little further to see its real cause. The relation sensed between a stone's fall and the moon's rotation around Earth in a fixed orbit led Newton to discover the law of gravity. Ever since this law received a general welcome, the cause of the falling down of an object thrown into the air has unquestionably been accepted as gravity. However, it is not necessary that the real cause of this movement be the force of Earth's attraction or the existence of another material cause.

Consider this: Two animate beings live on a two-dimensional table. They are aware only of this table and thus totally unaware of the three-dimensional world around them. Someone from the three-dimensional world throws items at the table in equal frequencies and causes holes to appear at equal distance from each other. Seeing this, these animate beings inevitably would conclude that each hole causes another one to be made, when in reality the causer of those holes is located beyond their world.

Those scientists who attribute every thing and event in the universe to the law of causality think that the universe works as follows: It is questionable whether the attraction of an object toward another one near it (e.g., the attraction of a falling stone toward the ground) is because of the objects themselves or because of some other source forcing the objects to such a movement.[3]

In short, an object that moves according to the law of gravity has each of its movements mathematically described and requires as many masses and distances as the particles in the universe and the distances among them to be known in their mutual, complex relations. Thus there must be One Who is the All-Knowing. This One also must have an absolute will to choose and assign for each event one law out of innumerable laws. The law's uniformity, meaning all the laws prevaling throughout the universe, calls for the unity of that All-Knowing and All-Willing One. The obedience of all things, regardless of size, to those laws shows that that One is also the All-Powerful. Again, the unchangeability or stability of the laws and the universe's magnificent, unchanging order and harmony show that that One is Self-Subsistent and All-Subsisting.

Given this, we say that this All-Knowing, All-Willing, All-Powerful, Self-Subsistent and All-Subsisting, and Single One causes a stone to fall, for only such a being has the absolute knowledge, will, and power necessary for a stone to fall. Every thing and event in the universe is too complex and magnificent for any material cause to bring it about. As a result of this truth, the only way open for humanity is to recognize God's Existence and Unity.

THE UNIVERSE IN THE LIGHT OF MODERN PHYSICS

Salih Adem

In the words of Einstein, "the least understood aspect of the universe is its being understandable." These words attempt to pierce the veil of habit that develops in our minds from not looking into the reason for things. The perfection of the universe's order is of such a degree that we are unaware of it, just as we only become aware of our watch's faultless operation when it stops working.

In the worldview based on Newton's laws of motion, the universe was likened to a flawlessly operating watch. Events were tied to one another in a cause–effect relationship, and our knowledge of this relationship's laws enabled us to predict events with great accuracy. We could determine with mathematical exactness a wide range of phenomena, from the times of solar and lunar eclipses to the amount of fuel and the speed needed to launch an object into orbit around Earth. The success of these "natural laws" led many people to believe that they completely expressed and "ruled" the whole order of the universe.

Our belief that causes are responsible for (or create) the effects is based on two factors: God creates and sustains all things and events from behind the veil of universal general laws, and certain events (causes) are followed reliably by similar events (effects) each time they (the causes) occur. But this is mistaken. No number of causes can create even a small effect, for every event, even the tiniest, presupposes the existence of the universe—including the laws operative within it. Moment by moment, all things and events are created and sustained by God, Who wills a particular actuality from an infinite range of alternative possibilities.

The clockwork model of the universe derived from Newtonian (classical) physics is not a complete account of the phenomena we observe in the universe. Already by the late nineteenth century, scientists were bewildered by the lines that turned up in the light spectra emitted by heated gases, for the steady, stable, and even distribution predicted by the clockwork model did not happen. Also, there were problems explaining light's behavior: Sometimes it made more sense as a beam of particles, sometimes as a wave.

Today we have a very different understanding of the universe. This shift in understanding began in 1900 when Planck[1] published his work on radiation. Planck worked for 6 years to learn why the actually measured radiation from hot bodies did not conform to the values predicted by the classical theory. He suggested that bodies radiating energy did so unevenly and discontinuously, as opposed to evenly and continuously, in tiny packets (*quanta*). So startling was this suggestion that Planck himself, despite confirmation by experiment, thought that he had solved this problem by some sort of trick.

In 1905, Einstein[2] published an article using the concepts of definite-sized packets of energy to explain how electrons are ejected from metal when struck by light (radiation). Classical physics had predicted that the voltage (measure of the energy of the electrons ejected) would be proportional to the intensity of the light (radiation). However, Einstein showed that it was proportional instead to the frequency of the radiation. The conformity of this explanation with experimentally observed results gained Einstein the Nobel Prize. (Einstein did not receive the prize for his famous theory of relativity.) The significance of these findings and theories was not fully appreciated at the time.

In 1910, Rutherford[3] performed a ground-breaking experiment. He bombarded a thin layer made up of gold atoms with high energy particles and showed that the atom contained an extremely small positively charged nucleus with negatively charged electrons moving around it. Following the classical physics model, these electrons should have been small particles orbiting the nucleus in the same way as the planets orbit the sun, steadily losing energy until they fell onto the nucleus. In other words, the atom should have been unstable. Again the truth did not conform to the classical model. Three years later, Bohr[4] helped solve the problem by arguing that the electrons must move in fixed orbits until deflected by the absorption or emission of a unit of energy.

Atoms emit radiation after various external signals and only at specific wave lengths. As Einstein said, every different color of light is composed of energy packets that are inversely proportional to its wavelength (frequency). Since the Planck constant (h) is very small, the energy of these packets is also very, very small. For example, a normal light bulb emits 1020 light packets (photons) a second. Each photon is created when an activated atom or molecule passes to its normal (basic) state. Thus light, which allows us to see and which is a basic building block of life, develops as a result of the motions (in wave form) of electrons. Classical physics could explain many events of daily life, but not those occurring on the subatomic level.

During 1910-25, physics fell into a state of confusion because many measurements were in conflict with and could not be explained by general theory. This led Pauli[5] to say he would rather have been a singer or gambler than a physicist. In order to explain the observations being made, the whole way in which physical events had been understood required fundamental revision by wholly new methods.

This was achieved by Heisenberg,[6] a 24 year-old physicist described by his teachers as a person who dealt with the essence of a subject rather than getting bogged down in detail, a person with powerful concentration and ambition. Perhaps his success can be explained by the critical perspective he developed through reading the works of such great figures as Kant and Plato, which was later supported with the sound knowledge he acquired from great physicists. Heisenberg, who relaxed from work by climbing rocks and reading poetry, said:

> It was around three in the morning when the calculations were completed and the solution to the problem appeared in front of me. First I experienced a great shock. I was so excited I didn't even think about sleeping. I left the house and, sitting on a rock, I waited for the sunrise.

Like other scientists who established quantum physics, Heisenberg was a philosopher–physicist. The philosophy he accepted and advocated that allowed him to interpret atomic events is explained in the following words:

> Even though it is successful with classical physics, the language we use to explain physical events in the atom or its surroundings is insufficient. For this reason, after making a specific measurement in a quantum system (for example, an atom), using that knowledge we can get a theory that will tell us what kind of results we can find in the next measurement. But it's not possible to say anything about what takes place between the two measurements.

What pushed Heisenberg to make such a statement was that the mathematical tools he used to develop a theory that could explain the observed discontinuity of energy in light and atoms were abstract concepts that had not been used before. In classical physics, the numbers we know were used to give value to matter's position, speed, size, etc. In Heisenberg's quantum mechanics, these sizes were expressed with infinite dimensional n x n matrices that enabled physicists to calculate the properties attributed to electrons (energy, position, momentum, and angular momentum) in an approximate way. Since these abstract mathematical expressions did not have an equivalent in everyday spoken language, they could not be approached through a classical understanding. It was observed that an experimenter could measure an electron's position by altering its velocity. This problem was formally expressed in 1927 in Heisenberg's famous Uncertainty Principle.

Independently of Heisenberg, Schrodinger[7] made another significant breakthrough related to devising a mathematical description of electrons. Inspired by de Broglie's[8] hypothesis put forward 2 years earlier about the wave properties of matter particles, Schrodinger developed a "wave mechanics" by which a particle's movement could be calculated. But the fundamental question remained: What were these strange and original "waves of matter particles" or "waves accompanying matter particles"?

The mathematical formulations devised by Heisenberg and Schrodinger are complementary in the sense that physicists use the one that best resolves the particular calculations they are trying to make. There is no formally distinct space between the scientists and the phenomena they are seeking to understand and manipulate. In other words, their means of observation and manipulation (the mathematics) in some sense *posit* (put in place) the very phenomena whose place (among other properties) they are trying to determine.

Alongside Heisenberg's concept of an infinite array of rows and points to plot a subatomic particle's position or motion, physicists and philosophers of physics began speaking of arrays of events or "stories" to try to explain, in something resembling ordinary language, the ideas they were handling. This cannot be described as a worldview in the way that Newtonian physics confirmed and sustained a worldview; however, it is a clear and distinct disposition that admits the incompleteness and uncertainty of human knowledge as a structural element of reality, instead of excluding God as the Force Who wound up the clock and then retired from His creation. In other words, the uncertainty is not a function of our present ignorance (to be relieved by future knowledge), but an actual constituent of the way reality is.

Quantum physics, at least figuratively and metaphorically, has become a vehicle for interpreting such concepts as matter, beyond-matter, energy, existence, and non-existence in a way nearer to Divine sources. It also has led many physicists to settle accounts with their conscience and turn toward God, Who is understood to be simultaneously transcendent and immanent everywhere in the universe.

RELIGION AND SCIENCE: SHARED RESPONSIBILITIES

M. Saif Islam

H uman affairs are affected by science, both directly or indirectly, in many ways. First, the technological achievements of science have so transformed the way people live that it is hard to imagine another way of arranging our lives. Second, science's influence on human life has affected people's minds. For example, we no longer believe in various superstitions that darkened the world in the past.

THE GOAL OF SCIENCE

The goal of science is to discover rules that explain the relationship between particular events and their aspects in the natural world. We usually refer to such rules as *facts*. More specifically, the goal is to find the simplest rules and thereby understand the mastermind behind our universe's wonderfully subtle design. Since understanding these rules enables a degree of predictive power, science can give us power over the forces of nature operative in the relationships we study.

Unfortunately, science can teach us only how facts are related and conditioned by each other. The aspiration toward such objective knowledge belongs to the highest of which human reason is capable. Yet it is clear that knowledge of what *is* does not open the door directly to what *should be*.[1] We can have the clearest and most complete knowledge of what *is*, and still be unable to deduce from that what the goal of our human aspiration should be.

Objective knowledge gives us powerful instruments to achieve certain ends, but the ultimate goal itself and the longing to reach it must come from another source. Our existence and activities acquire meaning only by setting up such a goal and corresponding values.

> The knowledge of truth itself is very little capable of acting as a guide and it cannot prove even the justification and the value of aspiration towards that very knowledge of truth. Here we face, therefore, the limit of the purely rational concept of our existence.[2]

SCIENCE WITHOUT RELIGION, RELIGION WITHOUT SCIENCE

Great scientists always have asked: From where will the ethics related to the use of science come? How can we decide what our goal should be? What is the best way for all human beings to be? Great philosophers and scientists have been bewildered by these questions. Some, like Einstein, have expressed their understanding memorably: "Science without religion is lame, religion without science is blind."

On the basis of his own very rich experience, Einstein claimed that science can be created only by those who are thoroughly imbued with the aspiration toward truth and understanding, and that the source of such feelings lies in the sphere of religion. He also advocated the kind of faith that proclaims that the rules governing the world of existence are rational and therefore comprehensible to reason. Einstein could not conceive of a true scientist without this profound belief. On the other hand, in his famous essay "Atomic War or Peace," Einstein captures the helplessness of the scientist to influence moral judgements:

> The atomic scientists, I think, have become convinced that they cannot arouse the American people to the truth of the atomic

era by logic alone. There must be added the deep power of emotion which is the basic ingredient of religion.[3]

During the course of the past 3 centuries, the world fell under the domination of Western culture, lifestyle, and modes of thinking. The world is now so influenced, both directly and indirectly, by the West that other cultures' contribution to the mainstream of world life is relatively negligible. So when we talk about the modern approach to science, we can discuss the Western approach as the sole representative.

Scientific knowledge needs religion to become a blessing for humanity. In the past, a number of scientists came to realize this but then were at a loss when they encountered a serious conflict between their faith and the results of their scientific investigations. The universal moral idea of a quest for objective knowledge owes its original psychological potency to the link with religion. Yet in another sense, this close link was fatal for moral ideas. The enormous growth of natural science strongly influenced humanity's thought and practical life. Looking at what happened in the West, we see that the gradual increase in scientific progress resulted in a gradual decrease in people's moral sentiments and attachment to religion. This general phenomenon was limited to the West, although there have been a few comparable individual incidents in the Islamic world also.

When Copernicus and Kepler[4] had to face the moment of truth, they chose a road that apparently differed from their religion. Feeling that they had to state what appeared to be the real case, for this would be more respectful of the Divine wisdom, they served humanity's intellectual integrity. Their standing against the Church at a time when the West's modern scientific spirit was still in its infancy and in order to save the truth was a great blow to the Church's dignity.

Since that time, an apparently irreconcilable conflict has existed between knowledge and religious belief, and most highly educated people increasingly arrived at the idea that (religious) belief should be replaced by (scientific) knowledge. Belief that was not based on knowledge was considered superstitious. This mentality engendered a negative way of thinking about religion. But the problem is older than this dispute. The root of Western belief was Judaeo-Christian and, long before science appeared in the West, the Torah and the Bible were corrupted by interpolations. As a result, the basic principles of Judaeo-Christian belief were so far removed from and irrelevant to the realities of nature and human affairs that it lost the right to claim any authority over knowledge.

Traditionally, there is a correlation between religion and morals. In the last few hundred years or so, we have seen a serious weakening of moral thought and sentiment. This has been the main cause of the barbarization of political and collective life in recent times. This barbarization, along with the terrifying efficiency of modern technology, poses a serious threat for human well-being.

The West began to study nature independently in the early seventeenth century. As a result, religion started to lose its influence on society. There was an effort to separate and secularize the whole domain of science. Unfortunately, this effort had the long-term effect of making science an enemy of religion, which lost its esteem among enlightened people. In time, great scientists arose without any knowledge of religion or moral values. Due to the numerous contradictions in the West's religious reasoning, the subtle influence of religious sentiments started to dry up in the minds of great scientists. Too many contradictory theories tried to explain the world. This is how science became (in Einstein's sense of the term) "blind" in the West: All means are no more than blunt instruments if they have no living spirit behind them.

Since that time, the West has focused its intellectual energies on studying a thing's quantitative aspect and thus developed a science of physical nature. The obvious fruits of such studies have won it great respect among people everywhere.

Most Western people identified science with technology and its application. They acquired the power of technology and used it to make life more comfortable and secure, to liberate themselves from the forces of nature. But science made almost no contribution to their moral or spiritual improvement. Just as natural science's success had helped people to dismiss religion as incapable of guiding rational thought, no authoritative source remained to guide people toward noble actions or aspirations. Thus science and technology became tools of domination directed against the rest of humanity, tools used to uproot other peoples, humiliate or destroy local cultures and beliefs, and to replace long-established socio-economic structures. Such developments have deprived many indigenous people of dignity, self-confidence, and direction.

SCIENCE AND EXPLOITATION

The [twentieth] century witnessed a depressing reality: the exploitation of most people by a scientifically well-equipped minority who believed that they had a hereditary right to control the world. This powerful minority had some internal divisions, with the result that the ensuing conflicts caused unparalleled suffering. Two world wars, aided by the most brilliant technological advances, destroyed millions of lives, deepened cynicism, and hastened the disappearance of traditional moral values in the West and throughout the world.

The power of Western science, despite any individual scientist's opinion, is on the side of a monstrously uneven distribution of the world's assets. Scientists say that even if the global population were to triple, everyone could be fed easily if technology were generously distributed and used properly. But the reality is frustratingly different: Millions die of hunger, malnutrition, or easily curable and non-fatal diseases; millions remain uneducated, live in miserable poverty, and have little hope for a better life.

People thought that boundless material prosperity would bring heavenly ease on Earth. However, it has caused endless complexity and a degradation of human life. Science gave us power to communicate over long distances, to see what was once unseen, to go where no one had gone before. However, it also took away our serenity and peace of mind and heart, damaged our aesthetic sense, and turned us into trivialized, emotionless, and mechanized creatures embarrassed to aspire to more than transient worldly pleasure or glory.

Theories about life are very abundant in modern times. Many are so contradictory that people no longer believe in the stability or permanence of what is good and true, and thus cannot construct a proper code of conduct. People question everything related to life. But their own finite abilities do not inform them of what they can and cannot know. Some questions that arise in our minds cannot be answered completely by our reasoning. Only religion can tell us something about such matters and guide us.

In the West, even those who think that religion should be given an esteemed position in society are not ready to let it dominate all aspects of life. They think that science can (and should) ascertain only what *is* but not what *should be*. Religion, on the other hand, can (and should) deal only with the moral evaluation of human thought and action, for it cannot justifiably speak of facts or relationships between facts. People see a potential conflict when a religious community insists on the literal or complete truthfulness of statements recorded in its Scriptures—in this case, the Bible. This is where the struggle between the Church and science (such as Galileo and Darwin) belongs. On the other hand, representatives of science often have attempted to reach fundamental judgments concerning values and ends on the basis of scientific methods. In addition, they have made themselves opponents of formal religion.[5]

THE ISLAMIC APPROACH TO SCIENCE

We now discuss the Islamic approach to science, its understanding of the relationship between natural laws (the truths into which modern science believes itself competent to inquire), and the truths of religion that, according to Islam, are accessible to reason and intelligible, even though they are mediated by Revelation.

To understand Islam's essential spirit, one needs an understanding of some of its fundamental principles, uniqueness, strong influence over Muslim hearts and minds, and vision of the ultimate goals of human life in this world and the Hereafter. However, it is difficult to express these ideas in modern terms to readers who are used to another way of thinking. To grasp this essential spirit, it is enough to recognize that God is One and that the Prophet, the recipient and means of Revelation and a symbol of creation, was sent by Him.

Islam has three levels of meaning. First, all beings in the universe are *muslim* in the sense that they have surrendered to the Divine Will. Second, all people who accept the Qur'an and follow the Prophet's Sunna[6] are *muslim* in the formal sense that they surrender their will to these two sources. Third, there is the Islam of the level of pure knowledge and understanding. This is the contemplative (Gnostic) level, which is considered the highest and most inclusive level of submission, when a Muslim surrenders completely to God and *reflects* the Divine Intellect according to his or her own degree. Given this, Islam conceives of *knowledge* and *science* in a way that is fundamentally different from the contemporary Western concept of outward curiosity about the outer world and analytical speculation to satisfy that curiosity.

Islam bases the arts and sciences on the Divine Unity that is at the heart of the Revelation. Just as the great works of Islamic art, such as [Islamic Spain's] Alhambra or Istanbul's mosques, provide patterns through which one can contemplate the Divine Unity manifesting itself in multiplicity, so do all Islamic sciences reveal the unity of nature.[7] The aim of Islamic science as a whole, and more generally speaking of all ancient and medieval cosmological sciences, is to show the unity and interrelatedness of everything in creation so that humanity may be led, through contemplating the universe's unity, to the Divine principle of which that unity is the image.

Unlike Western science, Islamic science seeks to attain knowledge that contributes toward the spiritual perfection and deliverance of those able to study. As a result, its fruits are inward and hidden and its values are harder to discern. To understand it, one must place himself or herself within its perspective and accept that its means differ from those of modern science. Although Islamic science did not bring about the degree (or kind) of material prosperity and insatiable desire in society engendered by modern science, its contributions in mathematics, physics, medicine, geology, geography, architecture, irrigation, medicine, and chemistry are by no means negligible. Even more importantly, all of these contributions sought to relate the corporeal world to Islam's basic spiritual principles through knowledge.

The fundamental principles of Islamic science are also at variance with those of Western science in other respects. For example, Islam says that nature is a fabric of symbols to be read and realized according to their meaning. The Qur'an is the counterpart of that text (nature) in human language. Both nature and the Qur'an speak about the Almighty's Power and Divine Unity. Understanding His Power is very closely related with the profound understanding of His creation.

Unlike other religious Scriptures, the Qur'an encourages all Muslims to read and understand nature. It gives hints, discusses some basic scientific concepts, and asserts the absolute truth of all of its verses. Bucaille, a French surgeon, acknowledged that the Qur'an contains no single statement that is assailable from a modern scientific point of view: "The relationship between the Qur'an and science is *a priori* a surprise, especially as it turns out to be one of harmony and not of discord."[8] In fact, this is why no Muslim scientist ever experienced a *crisis of faith* or *moment of truth* similar to those experienced by Copernicus, Galileo, and others.

"BELIEVE IN ORDER TO UNDERSTAND"

Islamic principles also say that science, as well as human knowledge in general, is to be regarded as legitimate and noble only if it is subordinated to Divine Wisdom. Muslim scientists would agree with St. Bonaventure's (d. 1274) axiom: "Believe in order to understand." Like him, they insisted that science can truly exist only in conjunction with Divine Wisdom. So an independent and purely rationalist approach could never dominate mainstream Islamic scientific opinion.

By contrast, under the influence of increasing rationalism, the West went through a series of actions and reactions—the Renaissance,[9] the Reformation,[10] and the Counter-Reformation[11]— that have no counterpart in the Islamic world. Being free of any normative or spiritual values and cut off from Divine Wisdom, the West saw the rise of a type of philosophy and science profoundly different from their medieval antecedents—a science of nature that concerned itself only with a thing's quantitative and material aspects.

We now turn to the major sources of inspiration for the cultivation of science among Muslim scientists. Dr Muhammad Aijazul Khalid of Damascus University says that:

> In contrast to 250 verses which are legislative, some 750 verses of Holy Qur'an—almost one-eighth of the whole—exhort the believers to study nature, to reflect, to make the best use of reason and to make the scientific enterprise an integral part of the community's life.

One such example is:

> You do not see in the creation of the All-Merciful any imperfection. Return your gaze. Do you see any flaw? Then return your gaze again and again. Your gaze comes back to you dazzled and weary. (67:3-4)

In a sense, this is the faith of all scientists, the faith that inspires them most strongly. The deeper they seek, the more is their wonder excited and the more their gaze (perceptive and comprehending faculties) returns to them dazzled. Everywhere in the Qur'an we feel an obligation toward knowledge and science when we read verses like these:

> Behold! In the creation of the heavens and Earth and the alternation of night and day—there are indeed signs for people of understanding. (3:190)

> We created not the heavens, Earth, and all between them merely in idle sport. (44:38)

Hirschfeld writes:

> We must not be surprised to find the Qur'an the fountainhead of sciences. Every subject connected with heaven or earth, human life, commerce and various trades is occasionally touched upon and this gave rise to the production of numerous monographs forming commentaries on parts of the Holy Book. In this way the Qur'an was responsible for great discussions, and to it was indirectly due the marvellous development of all branches of science in the Muslim world. This again not only affected the Arabs, but also induced Jewish philosophers to treat metaphysical and religious questions after Arab methods.
>
> Spiritual activity once aroused within Islamic bounds was not confined to theological speculations alone. Acquaintance with the philosophical, astronomical and medical writings of the Greeks led to the pursuance of these studies. In the descriptive revelations Muhammad repeatedly calls attention to the movement of the heavenly bodies, as parts of the miracle of God forced into the service of man and therefore not to be worshipped.[12]

Muslim minds tried to discover the physical principles governing the universe because such an undertaking is part of their obligatory worship. This obligation is made so clear in the Qur'an that the Golden Age of Islam was characterized by the widespread nature of science throughout society. Brian Stock has remarked in his perceptive review *Science and Technology and Economic Progress in the Early Middle Ages* that:

> The most remarkable feature is ... that science in one form or another was the part-time or full-time occupation of such a large a number of intellectuals—most of these men were not scientists, they were universalists, physicians, astronomers, lexicographers, poets and even theologians at the same time.

After Christianity was established in the West, the areas under its control descended into barbarism. Yet just 2 centuries after the Prophet, the Islamic world under the Caliph Harun al-Rashid (ruled 786-809) was far more culturally active than the contemporaneous world of Charlemagne (ruled 768-814), although the latter started earlier. At the time when the Church restricted scientific development, a large number of studies and discoveries were being made at Islamic universities.

Sarton, a professor in the history of science at Harvard University, stated in his *The Life of Science* that the foundations of modern science were laid by the Mesopotamian civilization (present-day Iraq), whose scholars and scientists were their priests. The second development in science came through the Greeks. The third stage belongs to the Islamic world's meteoric rise. Its civilization, stretching from Spain to India, led the scientific world as the vast majority of past knowledge was exchanged between Muslim scholars and advanced with new discoveries and ideas. Beginning about the eleventh century, scholars in the Christian world spent nearly 200 years translating Arabic texts into Latin. Thus Islam paved the way for the Renaissance, which in turn led to science's fourth great development in the modern world.[13]

During these 400 years, for the first time in history science assumed an international character in the Islamic world's universities. Muslims of that time were more steeped in the religious spirit than they are today, which proves that Islam neither inhibits nor prevents the best educated people of the age from being both believers and scientists. Scientific knowledge was the twin of religious knowledge, and there was no reason for this relationship to end.

During the twentieth century, most Muslim reformers tried to preach the full message of the Qur'an. They did not call for restricting Muslims to religious knowledge, for they understood that the Islamic world's neglect of science had caused Muslims to drop out of the intellectual mainstream and, over time, lose their ideological, social, and political superiority. The great Turkish scholar Said Nursi asserted that the success of contemporary Muslims in exalting God's Word will be proportional to their advances in science, technology, and civilization. He indicated the importance of science by saying:

> For the Muslims it is a great adventure that the West has acquired science and knowledge, and Islam can therefore appeal to them more easily than at any time before.[14]

In fact, Said Nursi is an example of a true, devout Muslim whose love for science is stated in his beautiful expression: "There is a tendency in the cosmos towards perfection. Thus the creation of the cosmos follows the law of perfection."[15]

A MENTALITY OF DOMINATION

Developed countries are trying to maintain a monopoly on the planet's resources and riches. Scientists and other intellectuals of the past are now the *private intellectual property* of the West. According to Sayar:

> Even though the developing countries need the help of industrialized countries to overcome the economic and ecological problems they face, the latter do not intend to share with the Third World "their" intellectual resources; in other words, they refuse to transfer technology and know-how, however great the

need for it. [Their mentality is] What is yours is ours and what's ours is ours.[16]

Contrast this with the opening of the first university in Europe at Cordoba (Islamic Spain). Knowledge spread throughout Europe from Muslim sources. In the prestigious scientific journal *Nature*, Ghiles raised the question:

> At its peak about one thousand years ago the Muslim world made a remarkable contribution to science, notably mathematics and medicine. Baghdad was in its heyday and southern Spain built universities to which thousands flocked: rulers surrounded themselves with scientists and artists. A spirit of freedom allowed Jews, Christians and Muslims to work side by side.[17]

In the Islamic world, scientific enterprise had an international character. Muslim society was very tolerant of those who did not belong to it and who had other ideas. Al-Kindi wrote:

> It is fitting then for us not to be ashamed to acknowledge truth and to assimilate it from whatever source it comes to us. For those who scale the truth there is nothing of higher value than truth itself; it never cheapens or abases those who seek.

So the goal of Muslim scientists was to reveal the truth, not to use it to exploit others, as has been done by Western nations in recent centuries. Muslims viewed it as humanity's common heritage.

In the twentieth century, many influential Western scientists understood that their civilization's approach toward science is sure to lead the world to catastrophe. Many tried to find a solution and, just in trying to do so, came closer to the Islamic approach. Many of them now think that religion should be given a chance to make its impact on norms and aspirations, while science and technology have become evil instruments in the hands of cynical Western commercial and political interests.

In the dark years of the Cold War, Einstein said:

We, scientists, believe that what we and our fellow-men do or fail to do within the next few years will determine the fate of our civilization. And we consider it our task untiringly to explain this truth, to help people realize all that is at stake, and to work, not for appeasement, but for understanding and ultimate agreement between peoples and nations of different views.

In 1990, at the Moscow meeting of a global forum of spiritual and political leaders, Sagan[18] urged:

Mindful of our common responsibility, we scientists, many of us long engaged in combating the environmental crisis, urgently appeal to the world religious community to [co-operate] in words and deeds, and as boldly as required, to preserve the environment of the earth.

A UNITED FIELD THEORY

This religion-oriented approach is increasingly referred to in the West. For example, we do not need to unify the fundamental forces (e.g., gravitational, electro-magnetic and strong nuclear) merely to understand how nature works. However, for the last 30 years of his life, Einstein tried to find a theory that would do just that. Although he could not find this "united field theory," he had a deep faith that these forces are different manifestations of one and the same entity. Hawking,[19] another brilliant scientist, has spent his life searching for a united and consistent theory that encompasses all mysteries of the universe in one set of equations. He says:

Then we shall all, philosophers, scientists and just ordinary people, be able to take part in the discussion of the question of why it is that we and the universe exist. If we find the answer to that, it would be the ultimate triumph of human reason—for then we would know the mind of God.[20]

Understanding (or "reading," as Hawking puts it) the "mind" of God was one of the aims of all Islamic scientists during the

Golden Age of Islam. This aim was the easier to pursue, for it was supported by the Qur'anic revelation. In the future, God willing, scientific curiosity will be wholly motivated and guided by the Message of God and thus truly become a blessing for humanity.

REFERENCES

- Bucaille, Maurice. *The Bible, The Qur'an and Science*. Indianapolis: North American Trust Publications, 1975.
- Einstein, Albert. *Out of My Later Years*. Westport, CT: Greenwood Press, n.d.
- Hawking, Stephen W. *A Brief History of Time: From the Big Bang to Black Holes*. London: Bantam Press, 1988.
- Nasr, Seyyed Hossein. *Science and Civilization in Islam*. Cambridge, MA: Harvard Univ. Press, 1964.
- Nursi, Said. *Hutbe-i Samiye*. Istanbul: Sinan Matbaasi, 1960.
- ———. *Muhakemat*. Istanbul: Sozler Yayinevi, 1977.
- Sagan, Carl. *American Journal of Physics*, vol. 58, no. 7 (July 1990): 15-19.
- Sayar, M. A. "Is Technology a Common Heritage of Mankind?" *The Fountain*, vol. 1, no. 2 (April-June 1993): 4-7.
- Sarton, George. *The Life of Science: Essays in the History of Civilization*. Free Port, NY: Books for Libraries Press, 1971.

WORLDWIDE CORRUPTION BY SCIENTIFIC MATERIALISM

Suat Yildirim

Materialism was born in the West in the mid-eighteenth century. Berkeley[1] coined this term for an unjustified confidence in the existence of matter. The term later came to be used to signify a philosophical movement or school that attributed the origin of existence to matter and denied the existence of anything immaterial. Materialism also may be used to describe a way of life that considers only the material pleasures of life and bodily comforts and neglects the satisfaction of spiritual needs.

Since natural scientists study only the visible world and follow a sensory and experimental approach, and since they tend to accept as scientific only those conclusions based on such methods, the modern scientific worldview is quite similar to materialism. Although some scientists might believe in God and the existence of immaterial entities (e.g., the spirit), the modern scientific approach is by nature materialistic. Thus we can say that scientific materialism is more dangerous than materialistic philosophy, for philosophical ideas can be set aside as theories with only a minor impact upon one's decisions and life. In contrast, people have to think, believe, and act in line with scientific conclusions.

Scientific materialism also has a considerable effect on how we conduct our lives. If we attach no importance to belief in a Day of Reckoning, in a Supreme Being Who sees and hears whatever we do, is aware of whatever we think, and will call us to account for our deeds in the world, we will pay attention only to secular laws and design our lives according to the requirements of a short, transient life. Furthermore, if *being scientific* means denying or at least doubting the existence of anything metaphysical, and if we accept science's discoveries as objective knowledge and religious knowledge of the spiritual realm as superstition, we have no alternative but to live as materialists.

Given this, scientific materialism and the practical materialism it produces are responsible, along with the birth of philosophical materialism and communism, for the global erosion of morals and spiritual values, increasing crime and drug addiction rates, the injustices committed by the strong against the weak, the ruthless colonialism continuing in disguised forms, and other modern social and political diseases.

Although scientific materialism does not deny (at least in theory) the existence of truths beyond the visible world, it accepts that anything immaterial cannot be known, rather than the idea that it can be known but is not known to us at this time. Materialist philosophers can discuss God's Existence or any other metaphysical subject. However, since scientific materialism argues that only material things can be known, it causes one not to think about immaterial truths. This attitude engendered agnosticism, the belief that only material things (as opposed to God or metaphysical things) can be known. Scientific materialism also caused the rise of most modern false beliefs and "mystical" practices, because it tends to explain immaterial truths in material terms and therefore reduces quality to quantity and the spiritual to the physical. We see this most clearly in psychology, psychiatry, and psychoanalysis.

Practical materialism, another result of scientific materialism, now is prevalent among all of the world's people, regardless of their religion or lack thereof. Most people mean *economic* development and the betterment of worldly life when they talk about development, and give precedence to worldly life. Since material wealth and resources cause rivalry and competition in interpersonal and international relations, not a day passes without some type of clash somewhere in the world.

Even if we leave out human values, lofty truths and ideals, and spiritual happiness, all of which have been sacrificed for the sake of material development, the modern civilization established upon scientific materialism has harmed humanity. The products of science usually are exploited by the great powers to consolidate their dominion over the world. In addition, developments in genetics, biology, physics, and chemistry threaten our continued existence. Modern civilization, as pointed by Said Nursi, is founded upon five negative principles[2]:

- Power, which tends toward oppression.
- The realization of individual self-interest. This pursuit causes people to rush madly upon things in order to possess them and gives rise to an intense rivalry and competition.
- The understanding or philosophy that the nature of life is struggle, and that this reality leads to internal and external conflict.
- The unification of people on the basis of racial separatism, which is fed by swallowing up the resources and territories of the "other" and leads to terrible collisions between peoples.
- The service it offers is satisfaction of novel caprices or aroused desires. This service brutalizes people (whether the satisfaction is real or not).

Modern materialistic civilization stimulates consumption and therefore gives rise to new, artificial needs that daily increase in number. Through the power of propaganda and advertisement to exploit such regrettable tendencies as "keeping up with the Jones," it imposes its demands upon people. The ensuing lifestyle, producing to consume and consuming to produce, destroys our sense of a balanced life and causes many mental and spiritual illnesses. Such a way of life has no room for spiritual profundity or true intellectual activity, for intellect is ruled by pragmatism and the "need" to earn more.

It is highly questionable whether scientific and economic developments have brought us happiness, whether developments in telecommunications and transportation have met our needs, and whether we have found true satisfaction and solved our problems. Our needs increase daily. People in the past needed only a few things to lead a happy life, whereas we continually feel the need to acquire new things. To satisfy each new need requires more effort and production, which, in turn, stimulates more consumption. This leads us to view life as a course or process of struggle, and gives rise to intense rivalry and competition. Thus it follows that since "might is right" in such a world, only the powerful have the "right" to survive. This is what lies behind such Western philosophical attitudes or such "scientific" theories as Darwinian evolution and natural selection, historicism, and the like.

Materialistic science is also responsible for the ongoing destruction of nature and environmental pollution. What a pity that nature, this magnificent book and this lovely exhibition created by God, the infinitely Merciful One, and presented to humanity to observe, study, and to be exhilarated by, is now viewed by many as nothing more than a pile of junk or rubbish. Even worse is its continued descent into what can only be called a wasteland or a dunghill. Air, that magnificent conductor of Divine commands, now is becoming a suffocating smoke and a perilous "whirlpool." Water, that source of life and other Divine bounties, is either a hazardous flood or forms desolate expanses of pitch. And Earth, that treasure of Divine Grace and Munificence, is a wilderness that is no longer safely productive and has become ecologically unbalanced.

We do not belittle or condemn scientific studies and what they have accomplished. On the contrary, we welcome them enthusiastically as the signs and confirmation of humanity's superiority to angels. The Qur'an states that God created people as beings who would rule on Earth in conscious and deliberate conformity with His commands. Since we have free will and are not compelled to do anything, for only these characteristics allow us to fulfill our function in creation, God has distinguished us with the knowledge of things and made us superior to angels.

So, we welcome scientific development and discovery as the result of this superiority. However, scientific studies can provide humanity with true benefits only if they are pursued within the guidance of immaterial, metaphysical, and God-given rules. Their goal must be to establish a civilization based upon the following principles:

- Spread the belief that right, not power, is the true basis of any true civilization. Right requires justice and balance.
- Encourage people to virtue, which is a spur to mutual affection and love.
- Develop an understanding or philosophy that the nature of life should be mutual help, which leads to unity and solidarity, and not struggle.
- Unify people via a common belief, shared values and norms, in order to lead them toward internal peace and brotherhood.
- Guide people to the truth. Scientific progress should be encouraged so that it can elevate them, through moral perfection, to higher ranks of humanity.

This is the civilization that the Qur'an proposes and urges humanity to establish.

MATHEMATICS IS REAL: WHY AND HOW?

Bayram Yenikaya

L egend says that on the door to Aristotle's[1] dwelling was written: "One who does not know mathematics cannot enter." I do not know whether this means that those who did not know mathematics would not be able to understand Aristotle or if it was simply a way to urge people to study mathematics. However, we do know that mathematics always has had an important place in any people's thinking and life. Pythagoras'[2] famous theorem is still taught in primary and secondary schools. Every century has contributed something of its own to mathematics, which is now a universal "language" studied throughout the world.

There are two major theories about mathematics' origin or essence. One is attributed to Plato,[3] and the other to the Formalist school. According to Plato, mathematics exists independently of humanity, and people discover its objective reality, just as we discover other "laws of nature," which we tend to call "Divine laws of nature." The Formalist school asserts that mathematics is a product of human thought.

THE LANGUAGE OF NUMBERS

To show the difference between these two schools, consider how they view prime numbers (i.e., 7, 17, 41), all of which can be divided exactly only by themselves and the number 1. Platonists argue that prime numbers exist independently of us and existed in infinite number before we discovered them. Formalists opine that prime numbers exist because we have defined them as such, and that it is meaningless to think about whether they are of infinite number or not. They assert further that numbers came into existence when human beings began to count. A well-known account of how this happened is that of a shepherd who used to put a stone in his bag for each sheep, and thus could find out whether any sheep was missing by matching each stone with a sheep. Later on, people began to give numbers different names and, since their two hands had a total of ten fingers, they found it easier to calculate by the decimal system. This was followed by the operations of addition and subtraction.

According to the Formalists, even the simplest mathematical operations, such as the four basic ones, consist of logical rules based on certain axioms. They say that we perform mathematical operations by expressing certain rules with certain symbols. For example, we take 5 and 7, a couple of signs whose meaning in the physical world is unknown, and put between them the plus sign, a third sign whose meaning in the physical world is unknown, followed by an equals sign. We know that we must write 12 after the equals sign, because the axioms and rules of logic that we are using require us to do so. This is just what a calculating machine does: It goes through the necessary operations without knowing what it is doing.

Let's suppose that adding numbers consists only of applying axioms or certain logical rules, and that it has nothing essential to do with the physical world. If we took our number signs and applied them to physical objects like stones and sheep, we should be amazed that, as if by a miracle, 5 and 7 stones or sheep added together (according to the same rules as $5+7$) results in 12 stones or 12 sheep. We would come to know that the abstract, conceptual realities in our mind correspond to physical realities in the outer world.

The renowned physicist Paul Davies[4] has stated that if we lived in a universe where different physical realities prevailed, in a space where there were not any countable things, we would not be able to make most of the calculations we make today. David

Deutsch claims that counting emerged as the result of experiences. According to him, we can do arithmetic because physical laws allow the existence of physical models convenient for arithmetic.

Feynman,[5] considered the greatest physicist after Einstein, says about mathematics that the problem of existence is a very interesting and difficult problem. When you take the third power of certain numbers and then add them with each other, you obtain interesting results. For example, the third power of 1 is 1, of 2 is 8, and of 3 is 27. The addition of these numbers gives the result of 36. The addition of 1, 2, and 3 is 6, and the second power of 6 is also 36. When you add to this the third power of 4, which is 64, the result is 100. The addition of 6 and 4 is 10, and the second power of 10 is also 100. When the third number of 5, which is 125, is added to this, the result is 225, which is also the second number of 10 plus 5 (i.e., 15). And so on.

According to Feynman, we may not have known this typical characteristic of numbers before, but when we become aware of such characteristics, we feel that they exist independently of us and before we discovered them. We cannot determine a certain space for their existence, for we feel their existence only as conceptions.

Let's take another example: Ibrahim Haqqi of Erzurum, a eighteenth-century Turkish Sufi, religious scholar, and scientist who discovered a way of checking an added sum's correctness that may still be unknown to modern mathematicians. In order to check or prove the addition, add up the digits of each of the two numbers we are going to add up. Let's add 154 to 275, for which we get the answer 429. Adding the digits of each of the first two numbers, we get $1+5+4 = 10$ and $2+7+5 = 14$. Then we subtract 9 from each of these two sums, which gives us 1 and 5, respectively. The third step is to add these two results together: $1+5 = 6$. We follow this procedure with the digits of the answer we want to check, namely 429, and again subtract 9: $4+2+9 = 15$, $15-9 = 6$. The fact that we end up with the same number (6) means that our addition was correct. This way of checking an addition exists independently of us. We did not create it; we discovered it.

Just as water could lift objects of certain weight before Archimedes discovered it, and just as objects thrown into air or a fruit disconnected from its branch fell before Newton discovered the law of gravity, numbers have many characteristics, only some of which have been discovered.

Physicist Heinrich Hertz says that we cannot help but feel that the mathematical formulas discovered so far exist out there independently of us. We know that these formulas existed before we discovered them, but we cannot determine a space for them. Mathematician Rudy Rucker thinks that there is, in addition to physical space, a space of mind ("mindspace") and that this is what mathematicians study.

Most distinguished mathematicians agree with Plato's view. Gödel[6] is one of them. Before Gödel, it was almost a generally accepted view that mathematics is a function of a working human brain, and that it consists of collecting the logical rules that we establish between the symbols of two sets. He argued persuasively that correct mathematical expressions have always existed, even though their correctness cannot always be proved.

Penrose,[7] another Platonist mathematician, believes in the existence of profound truths or realities in mathematical conceptions beyond the thoughts of mathematicians. Human thought is directed to extend into these eternal realities, which are there to be discovered as mathematical facts by anyone. Penrose cites complex numbers as an example. According to him, these numbers contain a profound, timeless truth. He cites the Mandelbrot set as another proof of his argument. This set reveals the fact that even the lines, twists, and shapes of mountains and clouds were (or are) formed according to certain mathematical formulas.

WHAT FLOWERS REVEAL

The Fibonacci series also reveals some interesting things. Named after the famous mathematician Fibonacci,[8] this series progresses as 1, 1, 2, 3, 5, 8, 13, 21, 34, 55, 89, 144, and so on, each term being equal to the addition of the previous two. That is, 1 and 1 equals 2, 1 and 2 equals 3, 2 and 3 equals 5, 3 and 5 equals 8, and so on. This is the series found in nature. For example, when we count the spirals formed of the seeds in a sunflower, we find that those arranged clockwise are 55, and that the others arranged counter-clockwise are 89. Both of these figures are among the consecutive terms in the Fibonacci series. They may vary according to the sunflower's size. For example, we may find 34 and 55 in a relatively small flower, and 55 and 89 in a normal sized one. However, the arrangement is always as consecutive numbers in the Fibonacci series. The spirals are arranged in pine cones in 5 to 8. We may encounter the same figures in the arrangement of tobacco leaves.

Another extremely interesting characteristic is found in the numbers of petals of flowers. A lily has 3 petals, while a buttercup has 5, a velvet 13, a dahlia 21, and a daisy 34 or 55 or 89, depending upon its family. It is impossible to attribute this miraculous arrangement to chance or ignorant nature. If the DNA of a sunflower or a pine cone determines random numbers for its petals or spirals, how can their correspondence with the terms of the Fibonacci series be explained? The ratio between this series' consecutive terms is nearly 7 to 4, the so-called "golden ratio" and known in classical art as the ratio most pleasing to the human eye. In order to explain the origin of this miraculous reality, we have to accept that flowers know what is most pleasing to the human eye or that the "Hand" of One, the All-Knowing, All-Wise, and All-Beautiful, is working in nature.

In short, Fibonacci discovered this characteristic in nature and showed that the universe has a mathematical order. In other words, mathematics is the branch of science that studies the universe's miraculous order that the Absolute Orderer and Determiner, One Who determines a certain measure for everything, has established.

NOTES

ISLAM AND SCIENCE: AN OVERVIEW

[1] Maryam Jameelah, *Modern Technology and the Dehumanization of Man* (Lahore: al-Maktabat al-Arabia, 1983), 8.

[2] Hujjat al-Islam Imam Abu Muhammad al-Ghazali (1058-1111): Muslim theologian and mystic whose great work *Ihya' 'Ulum al-Din* (The Revival of the Religious Sciences) made Sufism (Islamic mysticism) an acceptable part of orthodox Islam. (Ed.)

[3] Imam al-Ghazali, *Fatihat al-'Ulum*, translated and quoted by Ignaz Goldziher in "The Attitude of Orthodox Islam Towards the Ancient Sciences," in Merlin L. Swartz, *Studies in Islam* (London: Oxford Univ. Press, 1981), 195.

[4] Jamal al-Din al-Afghani (1838-97): Muslim politician, political agitator, and journalist whose belief in the potency of a revived Islamic civilization in the face of European domination significantly influenced the development of Muslim thought in the nineteenth and early twentieth centuries. (Ed.)

[5] Keddie, Nikki R., *An Islamic Response to Imperialism* (Berkeley: University of California Press, 1983), 107.

[6] Seyed Ahmad Khan (1817-98): Muslim educator, jurist, author, founder of Aligarh's Anglo-Mohammedan Oriental College, and the main driving force behind the revival of Indian Islam in the late nineteenth century. (Ed.) Al-Afghani and Khan agreed on this point, but were bitter opponents elsewhere. Al-Afghani accused Khan of selling Islam to the British.

[7] W. T. Barry, *Sources of Indian Traditions* (New York: Columbia Univ. Press, 1958), 743.

[8] Ziyauddin Sardar, *Explorations in Islamic Science* (London: Mansell, 1989), 2.

[9] In any publication dealing with Prophet Muhammad, his name or title is followed by "upon him be peace and blessings," to show our respect for him and because it is a religious requirement. For his Companions and other illustrious Muslims: "May God be pleased with him (or her)" is used. However, as this might be distracting to non-Muslim readers, these phrases do not appear in this book, on the understanding that they are assumed and that no disrespect is intended. (Ed.)

[10] For example, see Pervez Hoodbhoy, *Islamic Science: Religious Orthodoxy and the Battle for Rationality* (London: Zed Books, 1991).

[11] Francis Ghiles, "What Is Wrong with Muslim Science?" *Nature* (24 Mar. 1983). For an overview of individuals and achievements of this period, see John David Yule (ed.), *The Concise Encyclopædia of Science and Technology* (London: Phaidon, 1978.)

[12] George Sarton, *From Homer to Omar Khayyam*, vol. 1 of *Introduction to the History of Science* (Baltimore: The Williams & Wilkins Co., 1927), 17.

[13] Hoodbhoy, *Islamic Science*, 85.

[14] Al-Khwarizmi (780-850): Muslim mathematician and astronomer whose major works introduced Hindu–Arabic numerals and the concepts of algebra into European mathematics. Latinized versions of his name and of his most famous book title live on in the terms *algorithm* and *algebra*. (Ed.)

[15] Sarton, *From Rabbi Ben Ezra to Ibn Rushd*, Vol. 2 Part 1 of *Introduction*, 176.

[16] Solomon Gandz, "The Source of al-Khwarizmi's Algebra," *Osiris* (Bruges, Belgium: The Saint Catherine Press Ltd., 1936), 1:264.

[17] Franz R. Rosenthal, *Science and Medicine in Islam* (London: Variorum Gower House, 1990), foreword.

[18] Al-Biruni (973-1048): a Muslim scholar and scientist who had equal facility in physics, metaphysics, mathematics, geography, astronomy, medicine, astrology, and history. During his travels in India, he learned Hindu philosophy, mathematics, geography, and religion from the Pandits to whom he taught Greek and Arabic science and philosophy. His scientific method, taken together with that of other Muslim scientists, laid down the foundation of modern science. He has been considered one of the greatest scientists of Islam and of all time. (Ed.)

[19] Seyyed Hossein Nasr, *Science and Civilization in Islam* (Cambridge, UK: Islamic Texts Society, 1987), ix.

[20] Hoodbhoy, *Islamic Science,* 149.

[21] Ali Abdullah Al-Daffa, *The Muslim Contribution to Mathematics* (London: Croom Helm, 1977), 37. See also D. M. Dunlop, *Arab Science in the West* (Karachi: Pakistan Historical Society, 1965), 11-12.

[22] Ahmad Y. Al-Hassan and Donald R. Hill, *Islamic Technology: An Illustrated History* (London: Oxford Univ. Press, 1986), 29.

[23] Hoodbhoy, *Islamic Science*, 77.

[24] Al-Hassan and Hill, *Islamic Technology*, 12.

[25] Sabian: A Southern Arabian trading people who originally worshipped planetary bodies but had embraced Christianity (the "Christians of St. John") by the time of the Prophet. They were considered among the "People of the Book." (Ed.)

[26] See Al-Hassan and Hill, *Islamic Technology*, 13, 60-70 for an extensive documentation of who developed whose ideas.

[27] Ziyauddin Sardar, *Islamic Futures: The Shape of Ideas to Come* (Darul Ehsan, Malaysia: Pelanduk, 1988), 157.

[28] Hoodbhoy, *Islamic Science*, 115-16.

[29] St. Augustine (d. 604/605): First archbishop of Canterbury, the apostle of England, and founder of the Christian church in southern England. His two most influential works are *The City of God* and *The Confessions*. (Ed.)

[30] St. Paul (10?-67?): First-century Jew who, after first being a bitter enemy of Christianity, later became an important figure in its history. [Although he never met Jesus or heard him teach], he became the leading Apostle (missionary) of the new movement and played a decisive part in extending it beyond the limits of Judaism to become a worldwide religion. (Ed.)

[31] Nicolaus Copernicus (1473-1543): Polish astronomer who proposed that the planets have the Sun as the fixed point to which their motions are to be referred; that the Earth is a planet which, besides orbiting the Sun annually, also turns once daily on its own axis. (Ed.)

[32] John D. Yule (ed.), *The Concise Encyclopædia of Science and Technology* (London: Phaidon Press Ltd., 1978), 245.

[33] Quoted in Hoodbhoy, *Islamic Science*, 27.

[34] Muhammad Jamaluddin El-Fandy, *On Cosmic Verses in the Qur'an* (Cairo: Supreme Council of Islamic Affairs, 1961. See pp. 20-25 and 330-37.

[35] Sardar, *Explorations*, 32-33.

[36] Maurice Bucaille, *The Bible, the Qur'an and Science* (Indianapolis: North American Trust Publications, 1978), 7.

[37] The Arabic word *hadith*, commonly translated into English as Tradition, literally means news, story, communication, or conversation, whether religious or secular, historical or recent. In the Qur'an, this words appears in religious (39:23, 68:44), secular or general (6:68), historical (20:9), and current or conversational (66:3) contexts. The Prophet used it in a similar sense, for example, when he said: "The best *hadith* is the Qur'an" (Bukhari). However, according to the *Muhaddithin* (Traditionists [scholars of Traditions]), the word stands for "what was transmitted on the Prophet's authority, his deeds, sayings, tacit approvals, or descriptions of his physical appearance." Jurists do not include this last item in their definition. (Ed.)

[38] Quoted in Sardar, *Explorations*, 34.

[39] Manzoori-i Khuda, "Creation and the Cosmos," *Islamic Scientific Thought and Muslim Achievements: Proceedings of the International Conference in Islamic Polity* (1983), 1:96-113.

[40] Afzalur Rahman, *Qur'anic Sciences* (London: The Muslim Schools Trust, 1981).

[41] Sardar, *Explorations*, 35-36.

[42] According to Ibid., 42, this theory may not be original to Khalifa. The Isma'ili mystic Ibn Hawshab al-Kufi used it to support the theory of the seven Imams plus the twelve Hujjats. But Khalifa popularized it and even substituted letters of the Qur'an to ensure that the theory worked. He often added a *nun* (*n*) and substituted a *sin* with a *sad* (two Arabic letters) to get 19 or its multiple. For a further discussion of his work, see Ibid., 37-42.

[43] Rashid Khalifa, *The Qur'an: The Final Scripture* (Tucson, AZ: Islamic Pro-ductions International, 1981), 177.

[44] Khalifa, 1985, p, 11.

[45] Khalifa, 1982, Preface.

[46] Khalifa, 1982, 88.

[47] Sardar, *Explorations*, 40.

[48] Ibid.

[49] Ahmad M. Soliman, *Scientific Trends in the Qur'an* (London: Ta Ha Publishers, 1985), 3. He maintains that the alleged conflict between science and religion was not a conflict between fundamental principles, but rather one in which some leaders were motivated by the desire to preserve their interests.

[50] Hoodbhoy, *Islamic Science*, 145.

[51] Ibid., 7.

[52] Ernest Renan (1823-92): French historian and critic. He began training for the priesthood but renounced it in 1845. Relativistic, concerned with fundamental problems of human nature, he studied religion from a historical rather than a theological point of view. (www.encyclopedia.com) (Ed.)

[53] Quoted in Keddie, *An Islamic Response*, 85.

[54] Charles Darwin (1809-82): English naturalist renowned for his documentation of evolution and his theory of its operation (Darwinism). His evolutionary theories, propounded chiefly in two works—*On the Origin of Species by Means of Natural Selection* (1859) and *The Descent of Man, and Selection in Relation to Sex* (1871)—have had a profound influence on subsequent scientific thought. (Ed.)

[55] Charles Darwin, *The Origin of Species* (London: Penguin, 1985 edn.), 458.

[56] Hoodbhoy, *Islamic Science*, 22.

[57] Ibid., 145.

[58] Seyyed Hossein Nasr, *The Need for a Sacred Science* (London: Curzon Press Ltd., 1993), 71.

[59] Hoodbhoy, *Islamic Science*, 145.

[60] Ibid., xii.

[61] Ibid.

[62] Ahmad Mahmud Soliman, *Scientific Trends*, 1.

SCIENCE AND RELIGION

[1] Quoted by A. Karim in *Islam's Contribution to Science and Civilization*.

[2] Pakistan Quarterly, vol. 4, no. 3.

[3] For these quotations, see Abul A'la al-Mawdudi, *Towards Understanding Islam* (Kuwait: IIFSO, 1970), 69-70, footnote 1.

[4] Abul-Fazl Ezzati, *An Introduction to the History of the Spread of Islam* (London: 1978), 378.

[5] Sir Thomas Arnold and Alfred Guillaume (eds.), *The Legacy of Islam* (Oxford, UK: Clarendon, 1931 [1947]), 9.

[6] *Indiculus Luminosus*, trans. by Dozy and quoted by Ezzati, *Introduction*, 98-99.

[7] Quoted by Ezzati, *Introduction*, 235-37.

[8] M. Fethullah Gülen, *Understanding and Belief: The Essentials of Islamic Faith* (Izmir, Turkey: Kaynak, 1997), 309-10.

⁹   David Hume (1711-76): Scottish philosopher, historian, economist, and essayist, known especially for his philosophical empiricism and skepticism. He believed that no theory of reality is possible and that there can be no knowledge of anything beyond experience. (Ed.)

¹⁰ Sir Karl Popper (1902-94): Austrian-born British philosopher of natural and social science who subscribed to antideterminist metaphysics, believing that knowledge evolves from the mind's experience. (Ed.)

¹¹ Rene Guénon, *Orient et Occident* (Istanbul: 1980), 57. Turkish trans. by F. Arslan.

¹² This took place under Emperor Constantine (280?-337), the first Roman emperor to profess Christianity (312). He started the empire's evolution into a Christian state, and provided the impulse for a distinctively Christian culture that prepared the way for the growth of the Byzantine and Western medieval cultures. (Ed.)

¹³ St. Thomas Aquinas (1224/25-74): Italian Dominican theologian, the foremost medieval Scholasticist. Although many modern Roman Catholic theologians do not find St. Thomas altogether congenial, he is nevertheless recognized by the Roman Catholic Church as its foremost Western philosopher and theologian. (Ed.)

¹⁴ Nicholas de Cusa (1401-64): Cardinal, mathematician, scholar, experimental scientist, and influential philosopher who stressed the incomplete nature of humanity's knowledge of God and of the universe; Ptolemy (flourished 127-45, Alexandria [Egypt]): Ancient astronomer, geographer, and mathematician who considered Earth the center of the universe (the "Ptolemaic system"). (Ed.)

¹⁵ See Erich Fromm, *Escape from Freedom* (1982), 70-71. (Turkish translation.)

¹⁶ Pitirim A. Sorokin (1889-1968), Russian-American sociologist who was imprisoned three times by the czarist regime. After the October Revolution, he engaged in anti-Bolshevik activities. He emigrated to the US (1923), and gradually became a professor of sociology at the University of Minnesota (1924-30) and at Harvard (1930-55). His writings cover the breadth of sociology.

¹⁷ Odysseus: Hero of Homer's epic poem the *Odyssey* and one of the most frequently portrayed figures in Western literature.

¹⁸ Martin Luther (1483-1546): German priest and scholar whose questioning of certain church practices led to the Protestant Reformation. He is one of the pivotal figures of Western civilization, as well as of Christianity; John Calvin (1509-64): The leading French Protestant Reformer and most important figure in the Protestant Reformation's second generation. The Calvinist form of Protestantism is widely thought to have had a major impact on the formation of the modern world. (Ed.)

¹⁹ Roger Bacon (c.1220-92): English Franciscan philosopher, educational reformer, and a major medieval proponent of experimental science. (Ed.)

²⁰ René Descartes (1596-1650): French mathematician, scientist, and philosopher; known as the "father of modern philosophy" because he was one of the first to oppose scholastic Aristotelianism. He began by methodically doubting knowledge based on authority, the senses, and reason, and found certainty in the intuition that he exists when he is thinking. Thus: "I think, therefore I am." (Ed.)

[21] God uses angels because the Dignity and Grandeur of Divinity requires that people do not attribute directly to God that which they find disagreeable and accuse the Almighty thereof.

[22] Seyyed Hossein Nasr, *Man and Nature* (London: 1976), 94-95.

[23] Jacques-Yves Cousteau (1910-97): French naval officer and ocean explorer, known for his extensive undersea investigations. (Ed.)

[24] *Sahih al-Muslim*, "Fitan," 110; *Sunan al-Tirmidhi* "Fitan," 59.

CAUSALITY AND THE QUR'ANIC WORLDVIEW

[1] According to Islam, these are the Qur'an, and the original forms of the Bible, the Torah, the Zabur (Psalms of David), and the "Pages" revealed to Abraham. (Ed.)

WHAT A FALLING STONE MEANS

[1] In this article, I do not consider such other essential forces as the electromagnetic and nuclear ones, which have a determining effect on a thing's movement. Expressed through certain mathematical formulas, these forces make movements in the universe even more complex.

[2] Said Nursi (1877-1960): One of the greatest contemporary Muslim scholars; often credited with preserving Islam in Turkey during a time of enforced secularization and official hostility toward any personal or social display of Islam. (Ed.)

[3] The event of attraction is the simplest event occurring in the universe. Just consider how a honeybee makes honey or a cow gives milk, events that contain far more physical interactions, chemical reactions, and cause and effect.

THE UNIVERSE IN THE LIGHT OF MODERN PHYSICS

[1] Max Planck (1858-1947): German theoretical physicist who originated quantum theory, which won him the Nobel Prize for Physics in 1918. This theory revolutionized our understanding of atomic and subatomic processes. (Ed.)

[2] Albert Einstein (1879-1955): German-American physicist who developed the special and general theories of relativity and won the Nobel Prize for Physics in 1921 for his explanation of the photoelectric effect. (Ed.)

[3] Ernest Rutherford (1871-1937): British physicist who laid the groundwork for the development of nuclear physics. (Ed.)

[4] Niels Bohr (1885-1962): Danish physicist who was the first to apply the quantum theory, which restricts the energy of a system to certain discrete values, to the problem of atomic and molecular structure. For this work he received the Nobel Prize for Physics in 1922. He developed the so-called Bohr theory of the atom and liquid model of the atomic nucleus. (Ed.)

[5] Wolfgang Pauli (1900-1958): Austrian-born physicist and recipient of the 1945 Nobel Prize for Physics for his discovery in 1925 of the Pauli exclusion principle, which states that in an atom no two electrons can occupy the same quantum state

simultaneously. This principle clearly relates the quantum theory to the observed properties of atoms. (Ed.)

⁶   Werner Karl Heisenberg (1901-76): German physicist and philosopher who discovered a way to formulate quantum mechanics in terms of matrices (1925). In 1927 he published his indeterminacy (or uncertainty) principle, upon which he built his philosophy and for which he is best known. (Ed.)

⁷   Erwin Schrodinger (1887-1961): Austrian theoretical physicist who contributed to the wave theory of matter and to other fundamentals of quantum mechanics. Co-winner of the 1933 Nobel Prize for Physics. (Ed.)

⁸   Louis Victor de Broglie (1892-1987): French physicist best known for his research on quantum theory and for his discovery of the wave nature of electrons. He was awarded the 1929 Nobel Prize for Physics. (Ed.)

SCIENCE AND RELIGION: SHARED RESPONSIBILITIES

¹   Albert Einstein, *Out of My Later Years* (Westport, CT: Greenwood Press), 26.

²   Ibid., 22.

³   Ibid.

⁴   Johannes Kepler (1571-1630): German astronomer who discovered three major laws of planetary motion: (1) The shape of each planet's orbit is an ellipse with the sun at one focus; (2) A quantitative explanation of how a planet's speed increases as its distance from the sun decreases; and (3) The relation between the average distance of the planet from the sun (the semimajor axis of the ellipse) and the time to complete one revolution around the sun (the period). These laws opened the way for the development of celestial mechanics, i.e., the application of the laws of physics to the motions of heavenly bodies. His work shows the hallmarks of great scientific theories: simplicity and universality. (Ed.)

⁵   Einstein, *Later Years*, 22.

⁶   The Sunna is the record of the Messenger's every act, word, and confirmation, as well as the second source of Islamic legislation and life (the Qur'an is the first one). In addition to establishing new principles and rules, the Sunna clarifies the ambiguities in the Qur'an by expanding upon what is mentioned only briefly in it, specifies what is unconditional, and enables generalizations from what is specifically stated and particularizations from what is generally stated. (Ed.)

⁷   Seyyed Hossein Nasr, *Science and Civilization in Islam* (Cambridge, MA: Har-vard Univ. Press, 1964), 35.

⁸   Maurice Bucaille, *The Bible, the Qur'an, and Science* (Indianapolis: North American Trust Publications, 1975), 110.

⁹   The Renaissance: Literally "rebirth," the period in European civilization immediately following the Middle Ages. Conventionally held to have been characterized by a surge of interest in classical learning and values, it began in Italy in the 1300s and lasted into the 1600s. (Ed.)

[10] The Reformation: The religious revolution within the Western church in the 16th century; its greatest leaders were Martin Luther and John Calvin. Its far-reaching political, economic, and social effects became the basis for the founding of Protestantism, one of the three major branches of Christianity. (Ed.)

[11] The Counter-Reformation: Also called the Catholic Reformation, or Catholic Revival, a period duirng the 16th and early 17th centuries when the Roman Catholic directed its efforts against the Protestant Reformation and toward internal renewal. (Ed.)

[12] Hirschfeld, *New Researches into Composition and Exegesis of the Qur'an*, 1902.

[13] George Sarton, *The Life of Science: Essays in the History of Civilization* (Free Port, NY: Books for Libraries Press, 1971), 146-66.

[14] Said Nursi, *Hutbe-i Samiye* (Istanbul: Sinan Matbaasi, 1960), 78.

[15] Said Nursi, *Muhakemat* (Istanbul: Sozler Yayinevi, 1977), 13.

[16] M. A. Sayar, "Is Technology a Common Heritage of All Mankind?" *The Fountain* vol. 1, no. 2 (April-June 1993): 4.

[17] Francis Ghiles, "What Is Wrong with Muslim Science?" *Nature* (24 Mar. 1983).

[18] Carl Sagan (1934-96): American astronomer and science writer. (Ed.)

[19] Stephen Hawking (1942-): English theoretical physicist whose theory of exploding black holes drew upon both relativity theory and quantum mechanics. He also worked with space–time singularities. (Ed.)

[20] Stephen W. Hawking, *A Brief History of Time: From the Big Bang to Black Holes* (London: Bantam Press, 1988), 175.

WORLDWIDE CORRUPTION BY SCIENTIFIC MATERIALISM

[1] George Berkeley (1685-1753): Anglo-Irish Anglican bishop, philosopher, and scientist; best known for his Empiricist philosophy, which holds that everything save the spiritual exists only insofar as it is perceived by the senses. (Ed.)

[2] Said Nursi, *The Letters* (London: Truestar, 1995), 2:310.

MATHEMATICS IS REAL: WHY AND HOW?

[1] Aristotle (384 BCE-322 BCE): Greek philosopher and scientist, one of the two greatest intellectual figures produced by the Greeks (the other being Plato). (Ed.)

[2] Pythagoras (c. 580 BCE-c. 500 BCE): Greek philosopher, mathematician, and founder of the Pythagorean brotherhood that, although religious in nature, formulated principles that influenced Plato, Aristotle, and the development of mathematics and Western rational philosophy. (Ed.) His theorem: The sum of the squares of the lengths of a right triangle's sides equals the square of the hypotenuse's length.

[3] Plato (428/27 BCE-348/47 BCE): Greek philosopher, the second of the great trio of ancient Greeks—Socrates, Plato, and Aristotle—who between them laid the philosophical foundations of Western culture. Building on the life and thought of Socrates, he developed a profound and wide-ranging system of philosophy. (Ed.)

4   Paul Davies, mathematical physicist and professor of natural philosophy at the University of Adelaide (Australia); recipient of the 1995 Templeton Prize for Progress in Religion for his efforts to resolve the science–religion dichotomy. (Ed.)

5   Richard Feynman (1918-88): American theoretical physicist, probably the post-World War II era's most brilliant, influential, and iconoclastic figure in his field. He re-made quantum electrodynamics—the theory of the interaction between light and matter—and thus altered the way science understands the nature of waves and particles. (Ed.)

6   Kurt Gödel (1906-78): Austrian-born U.S. mathematician, logician, and author of Gödel's proof, which states that within any rigidly logical mathematical system there are propositions (or questions) that cannot be proved or disproved on the basis of the axioms within that system. (Ed.)

7   Roger Penrose: (1931-): British mathematician and relativist who, in the 1960s, calculated many of the basic features of black holes. (Ed.)

8   Leonardo Fibonacci (c. 1170-d. after 1240): Medieval Italian mathematician who wrote *Liber Abaci* (1202: *Book of the Abacus*), the first European work on Indian and Arabian mathematics. Known in English as Leonardo of Pisa. (Ed.)

INDEX

A

Abu al-Faraj 'Abdullah Tayyib, 6
Abu Hayyan al-Andalusi, 76
Abu Ishaq al-Shabati, 15
Abu Ja'far ibn al-Zubayr, 76
al-Afghani, Jamal al-Din, 124
agnosticism, 35, 51, 53, 115
Ahmad, Kassim, 16
Ak Shamsaddin, 52, 57
Alhambra, 105
al-Hassan, 6, 7, 8, 125
al-Muradi, 6, 26
al-Razi, 7, 10
Andalusia, 36, 37
Antiquity, 6, 36, 37
Apollonios, 5
Archimedes, 5, 122
Aristotelians, 11
Aristotle, 8, 88, 119, 131
Assyrians, 55
Azizul-Hassan Abbasi, 13

B

Bacon, Roger, 37, 38, 128
Baghdad, 4, 6, 7, 29, 30, 111
Banu Musa brothers, 6, 7
Barberni, Maffe, the Cardinal , 11
Bashiruddin Mahmood, 15
Bayt al-Hikmah, 7

Berkeley, George, 114, 124, 131
Bible, 13, 14, 31, 37, 39, 55, 102, 104, 113, 126, 129, 130
Big Bang, 13, 14, 82, 113, 131
bio-medical ethics, viii
Biruni, 5, 8, 27, 29, 125
Bohr, Niels, 95, 129
Bologna, 10
Briffault, Robert, 30
Broglie, Louis Victor de, 97, 130
Bucaille, Maurice, 13, 14, 21, 27, 106, 113, 126, 130

C

Calvin, 39, 128, 131
capitalism, 40
Cartesian dualism, 49, 50, 51
Cathedral of Frauenburg, 10
Causality, 33, 59, 78, 79, 80, 81, 82, 83, 84, 85, 86, 87, 92, 129
Centrifuge and artesian wells, 70
Christian dogma, 39
Christianity, 9, 29, 32, 33, 36, 38, 46, 49, 51, 109, 125, 126, 128, 131
Church, 9, 10, 11, 18, 28, 31, 36, 37, 38, 39, 40, 45, 46, 101, 104, 109, 125, 128, 131
Clement VII, the Pope, 10
cloning, viii
Cold War, 111

colonialism, 36, 40, 41, 54, 115
Copernican revolution, 10
Copernicus, 10, 20, 46, 101, 106, 126
Cordoba, 29, 31, 111
cosmology, 12, 20
Counter-Reformation, 107, 131
Cousteau, Jacques, 68, 129
Crusades, 30, 36, 87
Cusa, Nicholas de, 38, 128

D

dabbat al-ard, 58
Daffa, Ali A., 5, 27, 125
Dark Ages, 29, 30
Darwin, 19, 104, 127
Darwinian evolution, 117
Davenport, John, 29
Davies, Paul, 120, 132
Day of Reckoning, 114
Deedat, Ahmad, 15
Descartes, 49, 128
Deutsch, David, 121
Diophantus, 4
Divine Unity, 52, 57, 83, 84, 105, 106

E

Egypt, 41, 128
Einstein, 35, 58, 59, 66, 93, 94, 95,
    100, 102, 111, 112, 113, 121,
    129, 130
El-Fandy, M. Jamaluddin, 12, 14, 126
embryo's formation, 62
embryology, 12, 14, 26
Enlightenment, 45, 49, 75
Enoch, 55, 69

Ephesus, 5
Epicurism, 36
Euclid, 5
Euphrates, 59
expansion of the universe, 65, 82, 83

F

Farabi, 8, 29
Feynman, Richard, 121, 132
Fibonacci, 122, 123, 132
fiqh, 42
Flood, The, 45, 55, 117
Formalist school, 119
Franklin, Benjamin, 10

G

Galileo, 10, 11, 37, 46, 88, 104, 106
Ghazali, 16, 29, 38, 124
Ghiles, Francis, 4, 111, 125, 131
Gödel, Kurt, 122, 132
gravity, 82, 88, 89, 90, 91, 92, 122
Greek and Roman civilizations, 5
Guénon, Rene, 35

H

Hadith, 14, 16, 27, 42, 74, 75, 126
halal, 23
haram, 23
Harran, 7
Harun al-Rashid, 109
Hawking, Stephen, 112, 113, 131
al-Haytham, 7, 29
hedonism, 37
Heisenberg, Werner Karl, 95, 96, 97, 130
Hill, Donald R., 6, 7, 125

Hirschfeld, 108, 131
historicism, 117
Hoodbhoy, Pervez, 3, 4, 5, 6, 17, 20, 23, 124, 125, 126, 127
Hubble, 65
Hume, David, 35, 128
Hunayn ibn Ishaq, 8
Huygens, 10

I

Ibn 'Abbas, 41, 72
Ibn Jarir al-Tabari, 57, 76
Ibn Mas'ud, 7, 41
Ibn Rushd, 7, 27, 125
Ibn Sina, 7, 29, 52, 57
Ibrahim Haqqi, 52, 57, 121
Industrial Revolution, 40
Iraq, 55, 109
Italy, 10, 130

J

Jabir ibn Hayyan, 5, 8
Jalal al-Din al-Suyuti, 41
Jameelah, Maryam, 1, 124
al-Jazari, 5, 7
Jerusalem, 71, 76
Jesus, 36, 71, 126
John Paul II, 11
Joseph, 55, 69
Judaeo-Christian belief, 102

K

Kant, Immanuel, 10, 75
Kepler, 10, 101, 130
Khalid, Muhammad Aijazul, 107

Khalifa, Rashid, 15, 16, 22, 25, 27, 126
Khan, Seyed Ahmad, 2, 124
Khayyam, Umar, 5, 7, 125
Khuda, Manzoori-i, 14, 27, 126
al-Khwarizmi, 4, 7, 29, 125
al-Kindi, 8, 9, 29, 111

L

Le Maitre, 65
Luther, Martin, 39, 128, 131

M

al-Majriti, Maslama, 7, 10
Malaysia, 16, 125
Ma'mun, the Caliph, 9
al-Mas'udi, Abu al-Hassan, 8, 10, 29
Massachusetts Institute of Technology, 5
Materialism, 1, 38, 47, 49, 54, 55, 84, 114, 115, 116, 117, 119, 131
Mawdudi, 18, 127
Mesopotamian civilization, 109
Middle East, 55
miracles, 17, 28, 43, 69, 70, 71, 83
Mohammed Abdus Salam, 24
Mongol invasion, 30
Moore, Keith, 14
Moses, 32, 70, 72
Muhammad, Prophet, 3, 8, 16, 28, 48, 124
mustaqarr, 64
al-Mu'taqid, the Caliph, 6

N

Nasir al-Din al-Tusi, 5, 7, 29, 52, 57
Nasr, Seyyed Hossein, 7, 8, 21, 22, 27, 57, 113, 125, 127, 129, 130
natural selection, 117, 127
Neo-Platonists, 11
New Testament, 32
Newton, 10, 35, 58, 59, 66, 88, 91, 93, 122
Newtonian physics, 97
Noah's Ark, 55
Nursi, Bediuzzaman Said, 91, 110, 113, 116, 129, 131

O

Odysseus, 128
Old Testament, 37
Original Sin, 39
Oswald Spengler, 77

P

Pauli, Wolfgang, 95, 129
Penrose, Roger, 122, 132
Pergamos, 5
Pius IX, the Pope, 10
Planck, Max, 94, 95, 129
Plato, 96, 119, 122, 131
Prometheus, 39
Protestantism, 36, 39, 128, 131
Ptolemy, 5, 10, 20, 128
Pythagoras, 5, 119, 131

Q

quantum, mechanics, 14, 82, 83, 96, 130, 131; physics, 96, 98

Qur'an, 3, 11, 12, 13, 14, 15, 16, 19, 20, 23, 25, 26, 27, 28, 29, 37, 41, 42, 43, 44, 45, 48, 52, 53, 55, 56, 57, 58, 59, 60, 61, 62, 63, 64, 65, 66, 67, 68, 69, 70, 72, 73, 74, 75, 76, 77, 78, 84, 85, 87, 105, 106, 107, 108, 110, 113, 117, 118, 126, 127, 129, 130, 131

R

Rahman, Afzalur, 14, 15, 126
Reformation, 107, 128, 131
Renaissance, 37, 38, 39, 40, 46, 87, 107, 109, 130
Renan, Ernest, 18, 127
Roman naturalism, 37
Rosenthal, Franz R., 5, 125
Rucker, Rudy, 122
Russell, Bertrand, 30
Rutherford, Ernest, 94, 129

S

Sagan, Carl, 112, 113, 131
de Santillana, 5, 8
Sardar, Ziyauddin, 2, 6, 8, 9, 19, 22, 27, 124, 125, 126, 127
Sarton, George, 4, 7, 29, 109, 113, 125, 131
Sayar, M. A., 110, 113, 131
Sayyid Qutb, 15
Schrodinger, Erwin, 97, 130
Shamsul Haq, 14
al-Shirazi, 7, 10
Sicily, 29, 37, 87
Soliman, Ahmad M., 17, 24, 127

Solomon, 70, 71, 125
Sorokin, Pitirim A., 128
Spain, 4, 30, 31, 36, 87, 105, 109, 111
St. Augustine, 10, 125
St. Bonaventure, 107
St. Paul, 10, 126
Stoddard, L., 30
Sullivan, J. W. N., 18

T

Taylor, Isaac, 31
Thabit ibn Qurra, 7
Tigris, 59
Torah, 102, 129
Travelling in the air, 70

U

Uncertainty Principle, 97
United States, 40
Urban VIII, the Pope, 11

V

Vatican, the, 11
Virgin Mary, 38
Vitruvius, 5

W

water-clock, 6, 26
Watt, James, 40
Weber, Max, 39, 40
Western civilization, ix, x, 6, 128
World of Qualities, 49, 50
World of Quantities, 49, 50
World War I., 77

Z

al-Zahrawi, 29, 52
zero, 5